The House & the Cloud

Building a Compelling Value Proposition Using Risk Awareness to Sell Technology

David H. Stelzl, CISSP

Stelzl Visionary Learning Concepts
Charlotte, North Carolina
www.stelzl.us

The House & the Cloud
Building a Compelling Value Proposition
Using Risk Awareness to Sell Technology

Stelzl Visionary Learning Concepts
Website: www.stelzl.us

Printed and bound in the United States
ISBN 1-4196-6618-5

Contents

Chapter 1

Why Sell Security?

Is security as strategic as everyone believes?

Security has the power to differentiate products,
increase gross margin and accelerate sales cycles.

In 1995, the average combined profit margin on my products
and services—heavily weighted toward midrange Sun Microsystems and HP UNIX servers—was about 38%. Whether you work
for a high-tech manufacturer selling your own brand of technology products, or you own or manage a solution-provider company
that resells computers or networking equipment, you're keenly
aware of what's happened over the last decade.

Every manufacturer in the high-tech industry is fighting to
maintain street price while working hard to sustain profit margins
for resellers. Meanwhile, resellers are trying everything from
packaging products and services, creating managed services
offerings and eliminating products altogether to grow the bottom
line.

Over the last year, I've spoken with hundreds of high-tech
salespeople, sales managers and owners of reseller businesses,
each of whom shares a similar story. Many started technology
companies 10–20 years ago, hoping to build a brand that would

provide high earnings as computer usage and complexity sky-rocketed in the 1990s. Many had technical backgrounds, with a vision to create something exciting that would yield riches beyond any technical or presales consultant salary.

Andy (all names have been changed to protect privacy) was a client who shared this desire with his father. With years of consulting experience under their belts, they grew their reseller company, partnering with giants like Cisco Systems, IBM, Hewlett Packard and Microsoft. Business was booming, so they hired technical staff, salespeople and administrative support to meet demand. Early retirement could have easily been the next step once they chose to sell.

Looking back at those times, so many companies enjoyed the same growth. But entrepreneurs find it difficult to relinquish anything when their businesses are prospering and have become an integral part of their lives.

While Andy and his father were building their legacy, another company was forming in the southeast. "Bob" and "Mike" were following suit, building their technology company around the growing trends with systems, storage and networking. They, too, had technical backgrounds, developing a company that outgrew most of their competitors. In 1999, they were offered almost $40 million for a company that, just five years earlier, had been a tiny startup.

Both companies grew, but neither sold. By 2000, Andy's company remained a 15-person shop. Bob and Mike, aided by a strong sales manager and professional services VP recruited from a larger global integrator, had morphed into a $75 million corporation with more than 90 employees. Interestingly, either company could have profited handsomely if it were sold.

Three years later, the tables turned. Both companies had become commodity resellers of server products. Bob and Mike attempted to speed growth by calling on large banks and pushing salespeople to boost volume. A year later, they were down to 20 employees and struggling to make a profit. They ended up selling the company for a fraction of the offers received by the end of the '90s, and they were forced to accept positions with their former competitors.

Andy, on the other hand, changed his business model.

What Went Wrong?

As Bob's and Mike's key players focused on the security value proposition (making security the pinnacle of all company efforts), Bob and Mike resisted this new direction, wanting to focus instead on larger systems and storage opportunities; as products commoditized, their company spiraled downward.

Tired of fighting with managers, their key players left to pursue their own entrepreneurial dreams, using the security value proposition they saw coming to light. Soon they became formidable competitors with incredible momentum.

Andy changed his business model. He moved toward what he now calls "total data protection," snatching business from commodity servers with thin margins. His extremely profitable approach incorporates data-protection and business-continuity concepts that drive many of the same products and services his company sold in the past.

This story is oft repeated by myriad company owners and salespeople I've recently met. Each had a great business, enjoyed growing sales, had prospects who took their calls and counted on early retirement. Then, as product commoditization took hold, the business declined—unless they were willing to do something radical. The hypergrowth of the '90s is over, and much of the cash that has funded the last seven years is running low. It's time for a change in business model.

Business owners are heading back to work, putting in 70–80 hours a week. Salespeople have limited access to decision makers.

Reseller companies are worth little in a strategic sale. Manufacturers are fighting to maintain a competitive edge as networks, storage products and servers commoditize.

Winning the War

So, how do technology companies fight against the forces of commoditization? And how does security create greater margins and the strong valuations required to profit?

Whether you're selling on the frontlines, running a sales organization, own part or all of a reseller company, or work on the channel side for a high-tech manufacturer, you need to understand security's strategic value and how to use its growing momentum to drive high-tech sales.

Is Security Truly Profitable?

It's no surprise that technology companies are struggling, but is security really a solution?

Over the last seven years, the technology industry as a whole has dramatically changed from a fast-growing, highly profitable business to one of thin margins and smaller bottom-line returns. In contrast, trade magazines tell you each year that security is going to be "hot." In 2007, *VARBusiness* once again reports security will be the No. 1 driver in IT—a speculation experts have asserted for the last decade. In fact, over the last 10 years, the purported trends remain the same:

- Every year seems to be the year of security.
- Every prospect claims to be increasing security budgets.
- Compliance promises big wins for resellers.
- Manufacturers demonstrate the problem's severity.
- Salespeople report few security-driven sales.

You may be among those companies that have actually jumped into the security boutique fray, or perhaps you work for or run an organization that has been observing the market, wondering how to enter the business. You may work for a manufacturer that has acquired security companies and is now asking you to focus on selling the new product lines. If you're a manager, you may be wondering about the kinds of people you'd need to hire, whether you're calling on the right kinds of clients, and whether you have the expertise to sell these products and services.

Most of the sales reps I know have been selling security appliances, but avoid higher-end security sales—a truism for both the manufacturer and reseller sides. Gross profits tend to be incremental and relatively low. Something obviously isn't working.

The Average Security Sale

If you sell security appliances, you've likely noticed stiff competition can delay a sale by months. You may be able to take your family out for a fast-food meal with your commission check, depending on your brand name, the brands you carry as a reseller and your product lines' margins. You're frequently asked to place an evaluation product onsite, using free installation services to get it up and running. Either way, the manufacturer claims the product installs "in minutes," so there really isn't much consulting business for this product, anyway. This hurts both the manufacturer (on the channel development side) and the reseller, who lives on gross profit. You conclude this may not be the right place to focus.

Perhaps you've been in a meeting in which security came up. Excited, you recommend a follow-up meeting with your security expert. In turn, he agrees to bring his expert, and the resulting meeting turns into a feature/function battle among existing versus your technology offerings. Again, you conclude this isn't worth the effort, so you return to commodity product sales.

Throughout the course of this book, I hope to change this cycle. Each of these issues is a symptom of treating security as a point product. By the end of this book, you'll understand why every client has a security need—and, by fulfilling this need, you can produce significant profits, regardless of your technology niche or the market you're calling upon.

While working with a Chicago group, I ran into Steve, an alumnus from one of my workshops. As I approached him, I could tell he was happy to see me. His words tell the tale: "I just turned an 80K opportunity into an 800K sale using the principles you taught us in your security workshop!" These are the same principles I'll share in the chapters to come.

It's not hard to sell security, but it does require a different approach—one you may not be used to taking. In the end, this book will give you a winning strategy for selling virtually any product or service by tying it to security.

First, let's take a look at the value you bring to your clients.

The New Value Proposition

What's your value proposition? How many times have you been asked, "What does your company do?"

It's a simple question. But the answer may prove more complex than you imagine. Consider the following scenario:

You're attending an association meeting, social gathering or group event. You meet someone new—perhaps an executive with a large manufacturing company in town. After striking up a conversation, an event organizer indicates he's ready to begin the meeting, and everyone is asked to be seated. Your new acquaintance quickly asks what your company does. You have only one minute before heading to your seat. What do you tell him?

Take a moment to write your answer on a sheet of paper. Underneath your answer, write a second sentence that explains the value your organization brings to prospective clients like the one you hypothetically met.

Each day, you meet people when calling upon the accounts you serve, as well as in meetings, gatherings or through prospecting. But how many of these interactions actually turn into long-term profitable relationships? How often do you have a value proposition that resonates so strongly that your prospect wants to formally meet with you or schedule subsequent meetings? If you're a manufacturer with a significant market share, you may have this value. For resellers, it's a different story.

Manufacturer	Reseller
Branded by products	Branded by partners
Tracking revenue	Tracking gross profit
High margin on product	Thin margin on product
Differentiated by product features	Just like thousands of other resellers

As a reseller, brand is associated with your product offerings. Perhaps you sell IBM, HP, Cisco or some other globally recognized technology. But in the eyes of a CIO, there are thousands of companies just like yours. When this happens, price becomes your differentiation—and it will eventually destroy your company if your business model was built like those of most resellers: high-touch salespeople supported by highly trained presales engineers or consultants.

On the manufacturer's side, new companies appear every day, looking to steal your hard-earned market share. The commoditization of your products cuts into profits and destroys your channel. Future success depends on maintaining a leadership position and strengthening your channel.

Selling commodity products does not offer a compelling differentiation story, unless it's based on price and delivery—much the same way wholesale distribution is modeled. Consider the trends in nontechnical industries like supermarkets, hotel chains and bookstores. These industries are investing in experience to change the way people shop. Customers no longer want to shop in a basic grocery store. Instead, they demand cafés, prepared foods, banking services and a florist. Security has the power to transform your company's offerings, if approached correctly. When leveraged correctly, it can create a value proposition that will completely transform business as you know it.

A Strategic Offering

Security may be the most strategic area in which technology sellers should invest. In my experience, security/risk mitigation leads the list of what buyers want.

Four Things Buyers Buy

1. Risk Mitigation
2. Operational Efficiency
3. Return on Investment
4. Competitive Advantage

Security ranks first because it's extremely difficult to demonstrate the three other priorities with basic infrastructure. High-tech manufacturers are capitalizing on this trend in many ways:

• In one interview, Cisco Systems' John Chambers stated he spends more than 50 percent of his selling time talking about security. It's one of his company's primary points of differentiation.

• Vista, Microsoft's newly released operating system, is focused on security, with many features from third-party security products.

• Juniper is leading its network efforts with security, while partnering with Symantec to build security into products.

• BMC Software recently added identity management as one of its eight key "routes to value," while focusing its messaging around ITIL (Information Technology Infrastructure Library), the new ISO 20000 standard that closely aligns with the ISO 17799 Security standards.

• EMC, with its recent acquisitions of RSA and Network Intelligence, has become a security company by adding access control and event correlation to its growing portfolio of security- and business continuity-related products.

• HP, traditionally a printer, PC and server company, is transforming into a software company and applying security, security management and ITIL (closely related to security) to change the HP brand. HP also boasts a very large security consulting division that works with enterprise customers to assess and remediate security issues.

• Citrix has developed from a remote-access company to an access-control company.

• Of the last 10 CA acquisitions, more than half have been security companies.

• IBM, with a recent acquisition of ISS, is increasing its security position with the XForce and ISS' global Security Operations Center.

Each of these companies' leaders has recognized that the products it sells are quickly commoditizing and that security has the power to create differentiation in the market. They know security is one of the four things buyers are buying and, in response, are building it into their core products, rather than leaving the job to third-party software companies.

Over the last six years, security is consistently No. 1 among IT expenditures, and for good reason. Throughout this book, I'll show you why it's the top priority, where the money is being spent and how to find funding for various projects, regardless of your customers' and prospects' budgets in the coming year.

A Growing Fascination

People are interested in security. If you hold a conference on help desk software, individuals who sit on or manage a call center will attend. They're not decision makers, but technology overseers. Advertise security trends and, if done right, you'll find the audience you target. When I work with resellers, I urge them to hold security seminars and then use security to sell any infrastructure in which their company specializes. Security has power as a value proposition.

I recently counseled a technology solutions company in the Midwest. (Let's call it ITS.) I worked with the president and a local marketing firm to mail personal letters to community business leaders. The letter described growing trends in information theft, current and future threats companies face, and the inadequacy of most corporate security strategies.

We planned a lunchtime event at a local restaurant, and I coached ITS' sales staff on how to turn attendees into clients, incorporating the principles outlined in this book. We reviewed the importance of data and the systems these business leaders rely on to run their business.

At the end of my presentation, I invited participants to a complimentary assessment from ITS. Fifty executives signed up to attend, 37 actually showed up, and 27 agreed to a follow-up meeting.

The combination of a compelling topic and a well-executed plan gave the ITS team more opportunities than a cold-calling campaign would have delivered over several months—even more impressive because the executives involved were decision makers.

Everyone Needs Security

If I could show your clients how insecure their data really is—and the devastating impact of theft or misuse—I'd have a selling opportunity.

Every company you're calling upon could be in big trouble in the coming months if management fails to take action against looming threats.

If we can identify this issue and prove the propensity for attacks, we have a sales opportunity. The sophistication of today's threats and the perpetrators of cyber-crimes change quickly, making most organizations more vulnerable than they think. The "bad guys" are winning, and the consequences range from personal liability to business failure.

Recent Better Business Bureau studies have cited identity theft as the fastest-growing crime in America, and child pornography is the fastest-growing Internet business. More than 100 million Americans' identity records have been exposed, according to a 2007 IDTheftCenter.com report. About 25 percent of my seminar attendees tell me they've been victimized.

Spam is also growing exponentially: More than 90 percent of all email is spam, and more than half may contain malicious code that could be used to take control of a PC.

While fear of losing information has not been sufficient to motivate executives to take action, justification of the extremely high likelihood of unauthorized access can. In reality, this is more than a standalone project; it's an infrastructure opportunity that can be enhanced and accelerated by using risk and security concepts.

To begin this process, it's important to understand cyber-crime trends, who is behind them and what they're doing to succeed in an environment where many companies assume they have acceptable security strategies. In the chapters ahead, I'll cover who to talk to, what to talk about, how to create the necessary justification and the technology areas your company should target to create a profitable business model. In effect, security can do several things for us as we approach the sale. In the remaining pages of this chapter, let's take a look at what security does for the seller.

A Positioning Strategy

In every workshop I've conducted, I ask attendees if they've met with board members for the companies they call on. In every session there's at least one—usually two or three.

Each time, they report:

- The meeting resulted from a strategic initiative, not commodity product sales.
- One of the four things buyers buy was involved.
- The meeting gave them a tremendous advantage with the account.
- In most cases, they were able to maintain relationships with higher-ups in the company, becoming advisors after initial contact.

I, too, have seized such opportunities. In each case, my security insights gave me access to the board. My assessments have frequently led to invitations to attend meetings, speak before associations and participate in strategic planning sessions.

Large manufacturers like IBM may automatically receive such access, but it's a rarity for the average salesperson. People want to know how secure their companies are. If they're convinced you can help them, they will invite you.

A Powerful Door Opener

Security is a powerful door opener. As a salesperson, I want to control the sales process, have an offering that truly matters to decision makers, shorten the sales cycle and maintain the competitive advantage. I want to become a trusted advisor to the companies I serve, ensuring our relationship is lasting and mutually profitable.

Security offers one of the most strategic positions for the accounts you serve. Your knowledge will allow you to become the go-to expert for companies that are trying to avoid information theft-related exposure, lawsuits, embarrassment, and fines. And because security intersects with IT disciplines like networking, enterprise systems, applications and telecom, various company departments will request your assistance with key business initiatives.

Security creates a new value proposition, offering greater access potential than any other product or service. Neither an engineering background nor a highly technical security background is required to sell/advise at the buyer level. (You'll want to have technical people to back you up.)

A Business Multiplier

With security's measurable growth over the last six years, why do so many companies fail to profit from it?

Companies approach security as a product sale, which raises all kinds of questions:

- Is there a return on investment?
- What is the likelihood we'll be attacked if we don't buy this now?
- How does this product compare to others we've seen?

This means the seller must justify the product, while facing comparisons to competitors and discount negotiations. The resulting installation is small, and the ultimate profit may not be worth the effort.

With minimal effort, however, you can use security as a value proposition, showing companies how they're being attacked and creating an opportunity where none existed. Over the course of this book, you'll gain an understanding of how to sell security to large enterprise accounts with big budgets and profitable ways to work with small companies that don't even have an IT staff.

While working with a global manufacturer over the last year, I found that most security opportunities involved only one product/install per customer. Only a fraction of this company's bookings came from 80% of its sales. But a few salespeople had figured out how to sell security, with more than 60 percent of security revenue coming from only 3 percent of the firm's sales opportunities. These talented professionals had discovered the right selling process—and you're about to learn the keys to making it happen.

Summary

- ☑ Security is a discipline, not a product.
- ☑ Security does not commoditize as products do.
- ☑ Security can open doors to an organization's highest levels.
- ☑ Selling security as a discipline can produce very large deals, while offering differentiation most products lack.

Chapter 2

Two Keys to Selling Security

How do you change the way people think?

The risk of losing its most valuable assets will drive a company's decision makers to purchase security solutions.

"We don't have a budget for these projects."

When I hear these words, I know I'm talking to the wrong people about the wrong things.

Companies reallocate when one justifies the need for security increases.

So, why is it so hard to sell security? How do we capture all the business we're hearing about?

Redefine Security as a Discipline

First, most companies that build products or implement security solutions have made a strategic error in defining security as another practice area.

Offerings like Voice over IP, storage solutions, enterprise sys-

19

tems, application development and security have encouraged technology companies to treat security as a product when, in fact, it is not. Security is a discipline.

Let's assume you're going to buy a car. Would you purchase one without security features and then hire a special auto security company to add the necessary products?

Years ago, when security simply wasn't part of the core infrastructure, a similar mindset might have been acceptable, but not today. While automobiles have many add-on security features, their basic structure includes safer frame design, panel design, security glass and meticulous engine placement to reduce injuries in head-on collisions. These security features aren't treated as post-sale add-ons. In fact, many consumers consider security to be their top priority when shopping for a car; just ask any Volvo owner.

Security is a discipline that must be applied to core products in the technology sector, as well. Cisco and Microsoft—companies that own the majority of corporate America's networks and operating systems, respectively—are working hard to build security into their products.

It's not hard to visualize every router and switch having firewall, intrusion detection, spam filtering and anti-virus software built into the network. And instead of installing several different products to stop viruses, spyware and spam, they could simply be part of the operating system. Just look at the marketing behind Vista, Microsoft's newly released operating system.

In the storage world, EMC outperforms all other providers, with twice the market share of its closest competitor, IBM.

What is EMC selling?

Security built into the storage process.

Security as a discipline does not commoditize in the same manner as a product like a firewall. In fact, analysts say the security appliance market has about five years left before it's built directly into networks' and servers' core infrastructure. Security appliances are a stepping stone to integrated solutions.

The Truth About Security Budgets

Over the last six years, IDC studies show steady spending increases in security hardware, software and services. Forty-eight percent of this money is spent on services, 33 percent on software and 19 percent on hardware.

As I write this book, 11.4 percent of the average U.S. IT budget is allocated for security projects, with most of the money used for policy and procedure changes or driven by compliance projects. This number will only grow over the next few years as cyber-crime threats escalate.

Eleven percent is a significant amount when you consider the total IT budget, but it's important to understand that security money is available from all corporate divisions—not just the IT departments.

A company's security budget often reflects how seriously it takes security. But don't let small numbers deter you from selling more. Utilizing the car analogy, what if I demonstrated that your transmission will fail tomorrow? Most of us haven't set aside a special budget for transmission repairs, but we'll come up with the money needed to replace the transmission or car. Even without a budget, we'll reallocate.

So, why is there a disconnect when it comes to security? Why are sales so challenging, margins so thin and sales cycles so long?

Many companies have told me that their products would sell themselves, compliance would drive big profits, and security products would be the No. 1 expenditure. But the appliance market constantly simplifies the process, and companies buy the minimum solutions as they experience fewer viruses and hacking. Decision makers have become numb to the news stories and warnings.

At the same time, a new appliance with a slightly different spin appears on shelves almost daily, saturating the market with cheaper, simpler solutions. Across the board, salespeople have become disillusioned with the prospect of closing big security deals.

The Two Critical Keys

There are two strategic keys to selling security. Focusing on them changes the sales process dramatically:

1. Take your focus off the product. Focus on the asset.
2. Find the asset owner.

When you focus on the product, your audience is the technical team. The asset is a business issue for decision makers—those with the liability and ultimate responsibility. Sales consultant and author Mack Hanan says assets are the margin-sustaining element of a business. The last person you want to meet in the selling process is the security person who has no liability. Security people are the influencers you'll engage later, once the deal is about to close.

In most meetings, you'll find two individuals: data (asset) owners and data custodians. We spend most of our time with custodians—the IT people that watch over IT systems. Identifying the owner is the key to making the sale. The custodian has no liability or real decision-making power, but salespeople mistakenly spend countless hours negotiating, proposing and convincing them to buy. I'm not stating that the custodian has zero influence, but never give him the task of selling your solution for you. He's an unqualified salesperson.

If you wind up in a meeting where both the data owner and custodian are present, you need to make sure your focus remains with the asset owner. If a technical detail comes up and the custodian wakes up, the decision maker may delegate the meeting to the custodian; the buyer has left the meeting. You'll hear something like: "Why don't you folks continue and Bob can fill me in later today."

At that point, the sales cycle is no longer under your control.

That's why it's critical to find the asset owner and begin the process of helping him preserve his business. Focusing on the product will sabotage your efforts, landing you a date with the data custodian.

Summary

☑ Security is a discipline.

☑ The first key to selling security is focusing on assets, not products.

☑ The second key is to find the asset owner/decision maker.

☑ Don't expect the data custodian to sell your solution for you. You'll lose the deal.

☑ When selling security, there are no budget constraints.

Chapter 3

How Secure Is Your Data?

Will your customers' current security strategy thwart the new breed of attackers?

Clients with important data also have security needs, even if they fail to recognize threats. Viewing this as a business-centric IT strategy provides the foundation for your value proposition.

Clients with important data also have security needs, even if they fail to recognize threats. Viewing this as a business-centric IT strategy provides the foundation for your value proposition.

In 2003, I had the opportunity to travel to South Africa for a two-day business meeting. With no time for sightseeing, I grabbed souvenirs at the airport for my wife and children. This was the only purchase I placed on my personal credit card.

About 20 hours later, upon arriving home, my wife greeted me at the door and informed me the bank had called repeatedly, requesting a return call as soon as possible. They would not tell her what the issue was, but indicated it was urgent.

"Mr. Stelzl, have you been in South Africa recently?" a representative asked when I returned the call. It seemed odd for the bank to know this, but I answered affirmatively.

"Did you purchase a large quantity of hydraulic equipment, in an amount approaching $25,000?" I was asked. "We have a record that someone made a card-present transaction of that amount just yesterday."

This meant someone in South Africa had actually presented a card with my name on it to a merchant and made a purchase. It was frightening to discover that someone at the airport had taken my card number and turned it into a credit card.

This incident occurred at the beginning of the credit card-fraud and identity-theft trend. At the time, I didn't understand how easy it was to duplicate a card, but today we hear about it almost daily.

So, how does this happen?

This chapter explores how cyber-crime has evolved over the last four years. While scaring clients into buying security has not proved effective, as a salesperson, you require a clear understanding of the security risks and how you can leverage them in your business.

The Changing Faces of Cyber-Crime

About 12 computers in an average organization encounter some form of malicious program (virus, spyware, botware or other malware) in any given week, according to CyberTrust, a firm dedicated to security consulting and managed services. About six sexually explicit graphics will be exchanged, and there's a 65 percent likelihood that a breach will involve someone on the inside.

These statistics highlight generally visible security problems, but they are not necessarily the most damaging. Managers would like to eliminate them, but are unwilling to spend more money than already allotted. In many cases, viruses have been handled adequately with antivirus applications with regular updates.

Since my trip to South Africa, credit card fraud has accelerated, and identity theft is the fastest-growing U.S. crime, as I've already indicated. The problem has escalated to information theft of many varieties.

Examples Close to Home

In June 2004, Brian Salcedo, 20, pleaded guilty to four counts of wire fraud and unauthorized access to a computer after he and accomplices Adam Botbyl and Paul Timmins used an unsecured wireless network at a Lowe's store in Southfield, Michigan, to steal credit card numbers. Salcedo and his friends first stumbled across the network the year before, when driving around town and using their laptops to locate wireless Internet connections (a practice known as "war-driving"). Upon finding the Lowe's network, they hatched an idea.

Working out of Botbyl's Pontiac Grand Prix, the group began working on ways to access key systems that allowed them to "skim" each card swipe as purchases were made at stores around the country, including California, Florida, South Dakota, Kentucky, North Carolina and Kansas.

The method of their attack was facilitated by the custom software Lowe's used to process credit card transactions. The hackers downloaded and modified the software, creating an almost undetectable tool for "skimming" card transactions.

On Nov. 5, 2003, Salcedo and his pals used a common Trojan program, readily available online, to gain access to Lowe's credit card transactions. Their modified TCPCredit program (the application used to process credit card transactions around the country) was unsuccessful at first, but they managed to "crash" several point-of-sale systems at the local store. These system failures alerted the Lowe's IT department to investigate, and they notified the FBI of suspicious activities.

Two days later, an FBI surveillance team observed Brian and an accomplice using laptops and two suspicious antennas mounted on their automobile, which sat in the parking lot. This time, the hackers' attempts to install the modified TCPCredit software were successful, and they began to skim credit card information as each purchase was made.

Later that evening, FBI agents could pinpoint what was happening by reviewing Lowe's log files at its North Carolina data center. Only six credit card numbers were actually captured that night, but had Lowe's failed to recognize that something suspicious was occurring, every customer might have been forced to order new credit cards.

Analyzing the Attack

This type of attack did not require genius. It was pulled off by a couple of young guys with the type of training provided to the average network administrator. The damage, however, was significant.

Salcedo's actions could have resulted in up to $2.5 million in damages (according to Lowe's reports), and he was sentenced to nine years in prison. But an even greater problem will continue to haunt Lowe's: its reputation.

One of Salcedo's friends eventually became a security consultant, as many apprehended hackers do. The unique aspect of this story? They were caught.

Not an Isolated Incident

In the last year, Citigroup had to notify 3.9 million customers that computer tapes containing their personal data were lost while en route to a credit bureau. CardSystems Solutions, a company few had heard of before June 2005, had allowed an intruder to break into its network, gaining access to more than 40 million credit cards. The hackers used a "skimming" program similar to Brian Salcedo's.

At the same time, *Secure Enterprise* magazine listed additional attacks, including unauthorized access to systems at Choice-Point, DSW Shoes, LexisNexis, Polo Ralph Lauren and several universities, including Carnegie Mellon, Boston College, Tufts and two University of California campuses. Ameritrade, Bank of America and Time Warner also reported losing data on tapes, exposing sensitive customer information like credit card numbers, social security numbers and other information that could be used to create fraudulent credit. The Identity Theft Resource Center posted the names of nearly 150 companies that reported ID theft in 2005, with 57 million exposed customers. By the end of 2006, this number had reached almost 200 with nearly 100 million exposed customers.

Many of these companies have well-planned security strategies, 24/7 monitoring systems, intrusion detection programs and other safeguards. But if data is unsafe with such large organizations— some of which are required to comply with federal regulations like the Gramm-Leach-Bliley Act—how can smaller organizations with limited IT budgets claim to have security "covered"?

The next time you're in a meeting with data owners and custodians, and the custodian announces "we have it covered," remind yourself of these statistics. Assume your prospects are either ignorant or lying.

Analyzing the Data

It's no surprise that banks and card-processing companies like CardSystems are targets, but universities are also at great risk. According to *USA Today,* students are prime targets for information theft because they have a limited credit history, take out loans, sign up for new credit cards, and often purchase cars and housing as they approach graduation.

Data analysis reveals 57 million identities were exposed in 2005, but only 8.9 million consumers reported being victimized by identity theft. What accounts for the discrepancy?

The hackers behind these crimes often keep a low profile, and they take more information than they immediately use. This means suspicious activity may show up on consumer accounts months after a security breach, so people must monitor their statements.

It's also important to recognize that some companies may not report losing data. In reality, 134 companies and 57 million consumers represent a small percentage of the real numbers.

Who's Behind the Attacks?

As a solution provider, your job is to understand how security crises occur and educate your customers. This means you must be observant, taking into account who is likely to misuse corporate data and where you may find them.

Customer ignorance is a boon to salespeople, notes Michael Bosworth, author of *Solution Selling*. When customers actually understand the problems they face, they frequently have a solution in mind, he says—one that any of your competitors can fill. It's also possible that a company has an internal network administrator who is working on the problem.

But when customers are unaware of the real threats—and you can demonstrate the level of risk they are facing—you have the perfect opportunity to act as a trusted advisor and promote the value of your solutions. Bosworth estimates 95% of the market is generally unaware of the big issues, allowing you to provide the necessary customer education. This starts with understanding who's behind the growing threat of information theft.

As defined by security experts, a threat in the ISC2 is "a party with the capabilities and intentions to exploit any vulnerability in an asset." Vulnerabilities, in turn, are weaknesses in the systems that hold a client's assets that could lead to exploitation. Risk is defined as the possibility of suffering harm or loss—in short, a measure of danger. All of these terms were defined years ago by military intelligence and law-enforcement personnel with expertise in counterterrorism.

When I served as director of security for a global consulting firm, I received call after call from security product manufacturers who wanted me to carry their product lines. Armed with the latest data, they were ready to show that companies could have been immune to attacks of the Code Red Worm, Slammer, Blaster and others if their products had been on board. It was tempting to remind them that if companies had simply kept their Microsoft patches up to date, this would have prevented worms from spreading.

Hackers and their techniques are a moving target. Understanding how the landscape is changing and who's behind the attacks offers clues to defending corporate systems. Corporate managers are frequently unaware of attack sources.

In the Lowe's case, the attack was opportunistic. Salcedo's friends claim they were merely looking for an email access point when they stumbled upon the Lowe's network. This may or may not be true, but they likely did not intend to steal credit cards when they first discovered the network. Six months passed before they actually started skimming data from the corporate headquarters.

Today's hackers have an ever-increasing bag of tricks for cyber-breaking and entering, and they're in high demand around the world for their industry expertise. In 2006, the *Wall Street Journal* ran a front-page story about a businessman who hired hackers to blackmail a company that refused to do business with him. Reports of organized crime-sponsored attacks have also become commonplace, with stolen identity information used to create money.

Spamming organizations are also paying big money to create spam relay services to market all kinds of annoyances, from Viagra emails to hardcore pornography sites. Hacking is big business for organizations that need money and aren't concerned with the ways they get it.

In the October 2004 issue of *SC* magazine, Ron Condon of Gartner describes the new world of hacking. The original hacker, he notes, was the "spotty 14-year-old who just wants to show off to his friends." The new world is composed of attackers—many from Eastern Europe or Russia—whose goal is much more sophisticated than the thrill of breaking in. "These people are in it for the money," Condon writes. *Network Computing* magazine reported in January 2007 that credit card and Social Security information can sell for as much as $10 apiece through identity thief-controlled Internet websites similar to eBay.

Organized cyber-crime is a relatively recent phenomenon, according to John Lyons of the United Kingdom's National Hi-Tech Crime Unit (NHTCU). "Three years ago, there was no sign of organized crime…this has only come to light in the past 12 months (as of 2004)," he writes. Organized crime members are developing relationships with hackers who are prepared to work for cheap rates to carry out the work of groups like Shadowcrew. Lyons says Russian programmers can earn 10 times the going commercial rate by switching to illegal cyber-activities, including credit card fraud, extortion, spam and even distribution of pedophilia materials. In the future, we should expect to see an increase in cyber-warfare activities.

What are these groups really after?

The Oct. 12, 2006, edition of *USA Today* exposed the real story behind organized crime. There's a $67.2 billion loss among victims of ID theft, and the organizations who steal this data are making a fortune. Four different companies have competed for this market; however, in the last half of 2006, an individual who calls himself the Iceman in online chat rooms took over the market by compromising his competitors' databases and stealing their information. It's ironic that a person in this line of work would get ahead by stealing from other identity thieves.

USA Today further explained that only about $8 billion was lost in virus issues—a minor loss when compared to $67.2 billion. It would be foolish for us to think this is just another virus or malware issue. This is a business looking to control a lot of information with a strong financial return. The problem is not really a technical one (viruses, hacking, worms, etc.). It's the realization that there's money to be made using data that's generally easy to obtain. Using technology, social engineering and the cooperation of disgruntled employees or strategically placed hired criminals, hacker organizations gain access to some of the most valuable resources within a corporation.

As mentioned earlier, it's estimated that a programmer can make up to 10 times his current income in some countries if he starts working for the wrong side.

Can you think of some people working in the companies you are calling upon who would jump at the chance to take that job?

Consider the IT administrator who missed out on a promotion and is now listing his resume online. The cyber-criminal discovers it on a valid job-posting website and contacts him.

What Are They After?

Today's cyber-criminals are after three things: money, identity and computer resources. All, in the end, focus on some kind of financial gain.

In a bank, money may be the target as programs skim money from accounts. But identity theft may also be used to generate money when names are misappropriated to apply for loans or create credit cards/other forms of credit.

Computers are needed to carry out the crimes that lead to money. Hackers may use a botnet used to infiltrate target systems, large networks of zombies can be used for spamming, and systems are set up for businesses that distribute child pornography.

The point is, these criminals are not using their own systems to carry out these illegal activities, but rather your clients' systems.

At some point, someone has to ask the question, "Who is liable for the crimes committed through these corporate-owned systems?"

Understanding Credit Card Theft

If you haven't already done so, visit shadowcrew.com.

Chances are you'll receive a message that states: "This domain is parked, pending renewal or has expired. Please contact the domain provider with questions."

Not much there, right?

But on May 30, 2005, *Businessweek Online* described this group as an organized crime operation that uses identity information to perpetrate fraud. The story reads like a movie about Mafia criminals, including Secret Service agents working out of a high-tech command center on a stakeout. Observed on 12 digital screens resembling a war room, the cyber-crime gang was being watched. Operation Firewall was created to track down and arrest a group of people trained in identity theft, money laundering and the resale of stolen information.

This investigation targeted a group called Shadowcrew, one of the first information-theft gangs to emerge, making illegal sites similar to eBay popular.

"At 9 p.m., Nagel, the Secret Service's assistant director for investigations, issued the 'go' order. Agents armed with Sig-Sauer 229 pistols and MP5 semi-automatic machine guns swooped in, aided by local cops and international police." The result: "Twenty-eight members were arrested, most still at their computers."

According to *Business Week*'s article, these groups are winning: "They are stealing more money, swiping more identities, wrecking more corporate computers, and breaking into more secure networks than ever before." The damages from these groups continues to grow into the millions.

Online information brokers like ShadowCrew.com take identity information and turn it into cash before account owners can react. It would have been easy for Brian Salcedo to take the Lowe's credit card numbers, visit "hacker" chat rooms and find brokers who, for the right price, would turn them into fraudulent cards. It's an astoundingly quick process that should not be underestimated, reselling stolen information for as much as $10 per line item—not a bad profit when you consider the millions of records being taken from today's corporations.

While it makes sense that hackers want to gain access to large companies, steal identity information and turn it into cash, it's not always easy to draw the same conclusions when dealing with the small- to medium-business (SMB) community. The risks, however, are real. The same people who carry out large-scale jobs are also attacking SMB companies.

How Information Is Stolen

Zombies are computers that have been hijacked by an unauthorized user and set up for future illegal exploits. The original owner remains in possession of the computer and likely is unaware of the second user; however, the system can be redeployed in an instant for new purposes, including acting as a relay for an attack against government resources, breaking into banks anywhere in the world or some other crime that could be traced back to the owner's system.

At this point, you may be tempted to think zombies or the malicious code behind these attacks is the problem, but there is more to it. It's a $67.2 billion business, run by people like the Iceman. It would be foolish to think that, with the release of Vista, Microsoft's new operating system, or perhaps Symantec's new release of anti-spyware software, the Iceman will pack up his business and go into something else. This business is expected to grow more than 20 times in the next three to four years; zombies are only a tool used today in the exploitation of data.

Well funded, the cyber-crime gangs after this data have the ability to pay off internal employees to do everything from installing malicious code on servers to hiring bankers to help launder money. Social engineering is frequently used to compromise systems by tricking end-users into installing agents that allow criminals to take control of their systems.

The simple act of opening up electronic cards or downloading free music and videos may be introducing bots into a system used to access corporate assets. Once the Trojan is installed, the game is over. The hacker is in and can do a number of things to hide from security tools that supposedly look for vulnerabilities and malware.

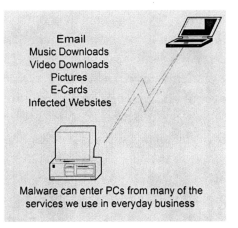

Email
Music Downloads
Video Downloads
Pictures
E-Cards
Infected Websites

Malware can enter PCs from many of the services we use in everyday business

Hired Guns

Businessman Jay Echouafni hired hackers and used a network of zombies to blackmail a Florida firm when a business deal didn't go the way he had planned.

Using a process called Distributed Denial of Service attack, these hackers were instructed to attack the target company's site, taking down its web server—a critical part of daily business.

Echouafni demanded a large sum of money to stop the attacks, which had caused about $200,000 in lost sales and system damage. By aiming a botnet that may have consisted of hundreds of thousands of compromised computers (zombies), Echouafni's hired attackers commanded their systems to make hundreds of thousands of requests against a single web server, a task most webservers are not equipped to handle. The result: an overtaxed server taken down by overload.

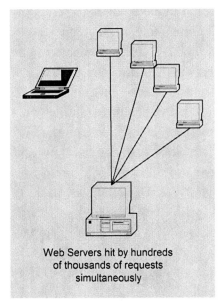

Web Servers hit by hundreds of thousands of requests simultaneously

Bots, or robotic malware, are used to create zombies,

35

building large armies called botnets. *SC* magazine reports more than 250,000 new zombies are created by hackers each day to carry out large-scale attacks. Over 7 million zombie computers form large-scale botnets around the world today. In fact, 70 percent of all spam emails are sent through these networks.

Imagine a worldwide network of zombies ready to launch a focused attack on a single entity, flooding it with so many requests that it crashes perimeter systems. Once a system has been hijacked, a Trojan is easily installed and the network is primed to take commands from the hacker.

Where Are These Zombies?

If you're wondering where all of these zombies are hiding, they're likely in the companies you call on, on corporate computers, laptops, home computers and perhaps even your personal computer.

The hacker's goal isn't notoriety; it's stealth resources and profitable crime.

In 2006 a study released by Microsoft revealed that an estimated 60% of all systems outside the corporate network contain botcode that may result in that computer being part of a botnet. Over 6% of all systems inside the corporate network are infected. This means that between outside systems in the form of corporate laptops and telecommuting PCs, and the 6% internal systems, chances approach 100% that your customers have zombie computers within their trusted network.

One retired FBI agent describes these attacks as "low and slow." Real hackers, he told me, were unhappy with the recent release of the Zotob worm, as it revealed advances in hacking technology from which criminals profit handsomely.

Attacks involving thousands of identities continue to yield billions of dollars. Hackers want to keep companies feeling safe while, behind the scenes, organized crime takes billions of dollars.

Everyone Is a Target

So, who are the real targets? In short, any computer that can be used in a money-making scheme.

Spamming is a growing, profitable market for those who take the time to figure out ways to get their message out without exposing the sender. Targets include any computer that can be easily accessed for use as a spam relay, computers that can serve as soldiers in a zombie network, larger systems that can provide storage/processing or any system that can be used to create money. Targets also include systems used to process credit card numbers, such as the ones Lowe's used in the skimming incident discussed earlier.

In the next chapter, I'll address the impact and associated liabilities that may result from these security violations. If you can prove cyber-criminals are in the accounts you are calling on, there will be an opportunity. Your understanding of what's happening in the world of information security—and how it impacts the corporations you deal with—will allow you to create the security value proposition message for the uneducated buyer.

With the right messaging, your prospects will take you seriously when you explain how identity theft has destroyed company reputations and customer trust, diminished shareholder value, eaten away at market share, and resulted in business failures, personal fines and even jail time. If you can prove to data owners that their systems are being compromised, you have a surefire business opportunity.

Take special note of one key point: If the data on your client's systems is not critical, there's no reason to call on him. Only clients who care about their data will spend money on infrastructure changes, application upgrades, performance improvements and safeguards. As a matter of fact, if data is not worth protecting, you are wasting your time calling on him.

But I'd counter with the following: "If a company has data that merits buying computers and networks, this client has data worth protecting." The question, therefore, is: "Does the client understand the risks involved in failing to take the appropriate actions to secure his systems and data?"

The problem, once again, is ignorance. The foundation of your security value proposition is client education: teaching him what security is and why he's a likely target.

Summary

- ☑ Security has changed. Don't expect increases in worms and viruses in the coming years.
- ☑ The motivation behind cyber-crime has shifted from notoriety and revenge to financial gain.
- ☑ Organized crime has figured out how to employ hackers to make significant money.
- ☑ Hackers' tools have evolved over the last several years, making older perimeter security strategies ineffective against today's botnets and automated attack methods.
- ☑ Most companies have been compromised. If the seller can prove this, the justification for the sale is there.

Chapter 4

Leveraging Compliance

How does today's growing list of regulations impact security decisions—and how do I leverage the momentum in compliance?

Making money with compliance requires more than an understanding of the regulations. Concepts of due care, policy and information life-cycle management trends can help you move toward the close.

Making money with compliance requires a new approach. Concepts of due care, policy and information life-cycle management trends can help you move toward the close.

In every security-sales class I conduct for resellers and manufacturers, I always ask, "Who has closed business in the last 12 months, with one of the federal regulations as the primary motivation for the client's decision to buy?"

In a class of 20 participants, I can count on there being one salesperson—perhaps two. Having taken this poll two or three times a week over the last year, I'm confident technology sellers are not making quota off the wave of compliance growth, save a few security-boutique consulting companies.

So, how important is compliance? And how should technology

companies approach compliance in the sales cycle?

Compliance is a major issue. Companies across the United States are working hard to comply with regulations, including Sarbanes-Oxley (SOX), Gramm-Leach-Bliley (GLBA) and The Health Insurance Portability and Accountability Act (HIPAA). (Note: Make sure you know the difference between a HIPPO and HIPAA, and that you don't try to sell HIPPA.) As companies take on these challenges, it's important for technology solution providers [manufacturers and the resellers] to understand who's driving these initiatives, how they will impact technology changes within the account, and how policies and procedures will be affected.

In this chapter, we'll examine some of the regulations, but we'll take a closer look at the real issues facing IT organizations and data owners. We will explore the significance of security policy and why it's critical for you or a partner to be involved in changes that will occur in the coming year.

The real value of compliance is that it has provided a heightened awareness among corporate leaders, economic buyers and asset owners. The growing number of new federal and industry regulations all seem to be focused on information theft and misuse, underscoring the growing threat against a company's digital assets. The bottom line: Asset owners are interested in security, risk levels and in gaining a better understanding of how likely they are to experience data loss or incur liability.

Addressing Compliance Versus Threats

There are several reasons a company buys security products, including a security breach or incident, an impending threat, an upcoming or failed audit, or an initiative to become compliant in a particular area. In each case, the sales cycle, buyer and buying process may differ.

In the case of an incident or impending threat, the sales cycle can proceed quickly. A company is suffering or sees financial consequences coming its way, so management spends the necessary money on security. But as mentioned in the previous chapter, companies are not seeing the majority of today's surreptitious attacks. The number of opportunities stemming from actual attacks is far too small to consistently make your quota.

With compliance, sales cycles are longer. But in the polls I've conducted, neither compliance nor realized threats have driven many of the security deals sold by the average technology solution provider. The exceptions are dealing with small boutique companies that specialize in security or small security-product companies that focus on some aspect of compliance such as PCI audits.

Compliance is often approached by committee. Most regulations are farther-reaching than a network, server platform or storage device. They involve business processes, personnel, training and a host of considerations the technology sellers will never sell or consult on. The committee is frequently led by someone other than IT—perhaps a compliance officer, department head, CSO/CISO or other manager. Whoever leads the committee, it's not a formal hierarchy as we know it. As such, whatever decisions are made are not the purview of a single individual. This, of course, creates a long sales cycle. Addressing compliance head on—unless you work for a highly specialized consulting firm or division that focuses on some compliance area—can be a difficult place to start.

It's no wonder companies are struggling to sell security. If your prospects don't see hackers infiltrating their networks or have auditors breathing down their necks, they aren't spending much on security. There has to be another way.

Where Regulations Apply

Almost every company has some regulation with which it must comply. Some are industry regulations, such as Payment Card Industry Regulations (PCI), which apply to all companies storing credit card information. Twelve items are specified on the VISA and MasterCard websites, similar to the 12 items required under VISA's original Card Information Security Program (CISP).

HIPAA, while closely associated with medical organizations, may also apply to large corporations that store patient healthcare information in company systems—for example, part of an infirmary, fitness program or employee assistance program. State and local government accounts will maintain HIPAA-regulated data (or patient healthcare information, known in the industry as PHI) through the school infirmary and prisoner health records. These are just a few examples to explore when consulting with clients.

Reading the Regulations

Unfortunately, reading all of the regulations proves to be a frustrating experience. Whether it's SOX, GLBA, HIPAA or another federal regulation, finding a specific infrastructure technology to sell can be a daunting task. Manufacturers and resellers have been using lines like, "We can solve 'X' problem with 'Y' product" for years, but none of these products is actually mentioned in the regulations, which are vague and complicated. They don't call for any particular infrastructure security solutions, making sales based on federal compliance a difficult and confusing task.

That said, a new approach is needed—one that does not require the seller to memorize the regulations (of which there are thousands), and one that takes the liability for compliance off of the seller's shoulders. This is how we'll address this market throughout this chapter. Instead of reading each regulation and putting in hours of research, let the committee perform this task. Let your clients' lawyers and department heads read and understand the data that must be managed under GLBA regulations, as well as where that data stays in the organization. Your job is to apply the appropriate security controls that deliver the level of security required by those who interpret the regulations.

One more important point here: Security requirements dictated by a committee to meet compliance laws are not equivalent to making a system secure. Additional security controls will likely be needed if the system is to be considered secure from today's cyber-threats. To simplify the selling process and create a faster sales cycle, I believe there are three key principles that can be applied to leverage the awareness and concern compliance have brought at the executive level. Through the remainder of this chapter, I will explore them.

Principle #1: Leveraging Due Care

Where there are regulations and data, there is liability. Find the data owner and understand his liability.

Use Concepts of Due Care

Due diligence and due care are two terms that are often confused in the disciplines of information security. I frequently hear them used interchangeably, but they are clearly different.

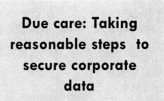

Due care: Taking reasonable steps to secure corporate data

Due diligence can be thought of as an assessment process. Many regulations call for a proper assessment of some kind, so it's important to conduct one. But liability is not associated with assessment. In fact, an assessment's scope is not well defined and therefore cannot be easily targeted for noncompliance.

Due care, on the other hand, is associated with liability. The data owner must understand what it means to demonstrate due care in guarding corporate assets, as well as the reasonable steps that must be taken to secure assets or data. Put simply, due care involves using reasonable controls to protect data. Per case law, if an incident lands companies in court, decisions regarding negligence in data treatment would be reviewed. The data owner would be asked to prove he took reasonable action steps to secure his data. An industry expert may be hired to define these reasonable steps.

If the case involved a manufacturer of bricks, the court might ask the expert witness about minimal requirements, and a simple firewall might be deemed adequate; however, if the manufacturer was involved in building weaponry for the U.S. military, reasonable steps would be far more stringent.

How Do We Address the Regulations?

I'm not a lawyer, so I urge salespeople to avoid addressing regulations directly. Rather, it's your job to educate the customer on due care.

Because regulations do not specify any infrastructure technology, moving toward due care is the safer way to go. In addition, regulations will change over time, as will threats. As your customers' security needs change, practicing due care and evaluating through due diligence will protect them from legal negligence.

In the coming chapters, I'll provide a simple way to look at security architecture to ensure due care is taken.

Principle #2: Applying the ILM Framework

Once the asset owner understands due care, you'll need to explain how digital assets work and the ways in which your products and services fit into the big picture of making an organization secure and compliant.

Over the last decade, storage companies have made the concept of information life-cycle management (ILM) a popular way to sell various types of storage. They've discussed it with executives and data owners, driving sales by emphasizing the need for different levels of availability, backup and recovery, cost per megabyte and distinct performance levels from various media.

This concept, now well understood by executives, can be leveraged in the security sale. In fact, ILM is really a security issue when you look at the creation of digital assets, where they are used and stored, and where they're disposed. One way to categorize your place in the overall security strategy is to look at the information life-cycle management stages.

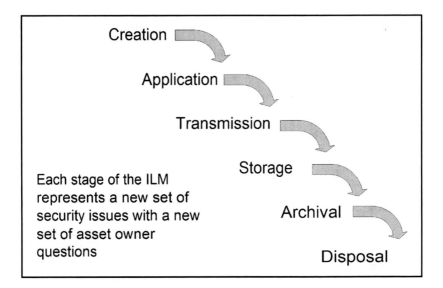

Creation

Application

Transmission

Storage

Archival

Disposal

Each stage of the ILM represents a new set of security issues with a new set of asset owner questions

Creation: Each digital asset has a point of creation. This may be an email, Word document, database entry, or even a phone call or voice mail message left on a colleague's phone. This asset has some value, which the creator or asset owner must determine and categorize as confidential or public information. There are many levels of classification; rather than exploring each, it is safe to say the asset must somehow be classified and used according to policies that govern this type of data.

Application: Most assets are associated with an application. This may be order entry records, patient electronic medical records systems, or a project plan or design document in manufacturing. The asset owner or federal regulations may restrict access to this information by stating who may view, change or delete it. The concepts of identity management come into play here to provide various users with providing authentication and levels of authorization to a given system.

Transmission: This is the vehicle for transporting data. LAN, WAN and wireless, as well as other forms of courier services, may be included in the transmission of data. Generally, this refers to networks and areas where certain assets can be transmitted, as well as the type of security that may be used to restrict access while in transit.

Storage: While in use, data is stored. Many of the assets we use in day-to-day business are stored in data centers, but not solely there. Data may be on laptops, PDAs or even as copies on web facing applications used by customers and suppliers. Data is stored in many locations; the trick is keeping up with data integrity and safeguarding it from unauthorized usage and theft.

Archival: Much of the data that comes from logs, communications involving financial reporting and email are saved for longer periods of time in accordance with federal law and internal policy. The process of archiving, securing archived data and maintaining data in a state that is recoverable becomes a concern as data ages. For instance, today a court may subpoena email data, and the company has 90 days to deliver that data. If your client was in this situation, would he be able to retrieve specific emails from five years ago? The likelihood is low, given the formats in which email is stored. Recovering data and maintaining its integrity require a good bit of forethought.

Disposal: Some data must be maintained for seven years, some for 99 years. But at some point, most data should be destroyed. When systems are outdated, and when PDAs and laptop hard drives are replaced, that data must be destroyed. Disposal is governed by policy, covering the liabilities associated with data that may later be in question. The last stage of the data lifecycle process introduces some of the greatest risk and liability. It should be well thought out before it's time to delete these assets.

I recommend you memorize these stages. It's simple to remember them if you use the acronym CATSAD. With these six simple steps, you have a framework to ask executive-level questions, beginning with the creation of an asset.

Sample questions might include:

- How sensitive is this data? Who is allowed to see it?
- Who has the authority to view it, change it, delete it or grant access to other users?
- Where are the applications that create or use it—and how secure are they?
- Where is this data transmitted? Is it used on wireless networks, sent through email over the Internet? Is it encrypted— or should it be? Are there various levels of security among the departments that create it or use it?
- How is it stored? How much data can you stand to lose? If your backups occurred last night and your system fails at the end of the next day, would you be able to recreate that data? For example, a construction supply company might be able to re-key orders from today; however, wire transfers or stock trade applications cannot afford to lose any data.
- How long does data need to be archived? If it is sent to off-site locations, should it be encrypted before leaving this facility?
- At what point is the information deleted? Do your policies state this, and are they enforced?

Make Sure You Understand Digital Assets

To secure data, it's critical to understand the difference between a physical asset, such as a chair or statue in the lobby, and the data companies rely on. The assets we are talking about are created every day: every email sent, voice mail message left on someone's phone, transmission of instant messages, spreadsheet created for tomorrow's meeting, orders sent by customers, new designs, manufacturing schedules or a PowerPoint presentation created for an executive overview. It's all data, and it represents intellectual capital.

If a statue were stolen, you would see it one day and it would be gone the next. In the data world, data is kept in large systems, behind locked doors. But with a simple thumb drive, this data can be copied from a system in the lobby or accessed from a parking lot. It can be stolen without the owner realizing it's been compromised. An attacker can change a few zeros and ones, turning millions of dollars into trash in seconds.

Further complicating the issue, the data no longer resides where we think it does: in the data center. My sales data, for example, is accessed through an online sales-force automation program; my accounting processes are run through an online accounting program; and the local copy of contacts and email sitting on my laptop is synchronized with a PDA.

Have you ever given away a PC or PDA to a charity or sold one online? If you did, you most likely erased your data, but didn't realize it's not erased completely until the disk has been formatted or erased seven times (according to government standards). Companies are losing data every day as employees leave and take it with them. Recent reports from security analysts indicate employees are finding ways to sell the data their company's prize. It's pretty easy to walk out with company secrets, which are worth a lot of money to competitors.

Using language with which executives are accustomed can help pave the way to connecting with senior management, and information life-cycle management terms are no exception.

Relating ILM Stages to Compliance Requirements

At each stage of ILM, security requirements change. Different threats exist, and appropriate controls are required. Looking at different ILM stages allows us to see what a regulation says about data each step of the way.

For instance, when data is created, it should be classified. This is something government organizations have been doing for years, but it's inconsistent among private-sector organizations. Many popular compliance areas seem to address these stages, specifying how applications should be treated and accessed, where and how information can be transmitted, specifications for storage and archival, and when data can be disposed of. Regulations will vary on these points, but your job is not to interpret them. You must take your clients' interpretations of each stage and ensure technology exists to enforce policies. Once again, by using the concepts of ILM, you have an easy-to-remember framework for asking questions at the asset-owner level.

> **ILM provides an easy-to-remember framework for developing executive-level questions at every stage of data's life cycle.**

For example, when HIPAA data is created, we're talking about patient healthcare information (PHI). In the GLBA regulations, it's customer account information. Both regulations require only certain individuals to have access to the data on a need-to-know basis; this is an application issue. Both laws prohibit data from being transmitted in an insecure fashion—especially outside the organization, in an unencrypted manner. This may impact the use of wireless network access or email.

If you are a network provider, you are providing the secure transport of digital assets. The asset owner tells you which data is subject to the restrictions, where in the infrastructure it resides, who accesses it, etc. Once this is defined, your job as a solution provider is to deliver the capability to meet the asset owner's demands. You are not liable for failing to interpret the laws correctly, nor should you be.

Your goal at each stage of the ILM is to provide the client with the technology and best practices that comply with the concepts of due care. When this is properly done, regardless of pending regulations, at an infrastructure level, your client should be covered (unless there are specific infrastructure-related compliance stipulations).

Principle #3: The Power of Policy

Policy drives architecture and limits liability. Most companies of a certain size seem to have a policy, but it often has little meaning to the organization. The power to limit liability lies in the enforcement and consistency of the policy. When a due-care issue arises or a violation occurs, the policy must be there to address it.

In 2006, AGFA reported the loss of thousands of customer records, which resided on a laptop that had been left in an automobile's backseat. The company reported the laptop had been stolen, but stated it was the result of an employee who broke policy and left the records unattended. In other words, the company claimed it was not liable for any damages resulting from data ending up in the wrong hands.

Policy drives architecture and limits liability.

Was the employee at fault, or was the company negligent?

If this case requires legal action, the employee would have to prove that the policy was actually a recommendation—not a formal policy. He can do this by showing that other policies have not been enforced and were treated as recommendations. If he's successful, the court may rule the policy was merely a recommendation, and the company would be liable for the loss.

Compliance Is Driving Policy Changes

The link between policy and compliance is simple: As compliance areas are addressed, companies are changing policy. They must do this to limit liability.

Policy drives architecture. It's critical that you, the seller, become involved in policy changes, as they drive new architecture requirements.

For instance, I was working on a policy for a hospital. The company-specified technology standards like OpSec-compliant products to secure the network's perimeter. But what if your company doesn't represent products certified by Check Point Software, the owners of OpSec compliance standards? While they sound like a government standard, they're not.

As I work with companies on policies, I find the standards often call for specific products, brands or industry certifications. If your company is going to assist with securing data, a standard may stand in the way. Policies and standards are not easily changed once senior management signs off on them.

This is why it's vital to get involved in policy changes. Make sure your organization is setting the standards, allowing you to drive the architecture.

What Happens When Companies Fail to Comply?

It's unknown what happens to companies that fail to comply. A simple web search indicates individuals are not going to jail, as mandated by many federal regulations. This, however, doesn't mean they will never face jail time.

What we *can* be sure of, based on history, is this: If a company has a major security violation and loses significant data, it will have to prove due care was practiced. Management will have to show reasonable steps were taken to secure the data. Data owners may also have to demonstrate that their systems were in compliance with federal and industry regulations.

If we look at the last year, fines have frequently come from the Federal Trade Commission, rather than industry enforcement through companies like VISA; on the federal side, the same is true. Fines levied against DSW and other retailers that allowed information thieves to gain access to confidential data came through the FTC, rather than auditors specific to California's SB 1386 (state law requiring companies operating in California to disclose data theft to their customers when the data exposes personal information like account numbers or even a driver's license number) or a similar regulation.

On the other hand, I'm aware of several large retailers that have failed to pass PCI audits and have refused to spend the money required to address their problems. Will MasterCard take away the privilege of accepting payments? It's unknown.

In 2007, VISA and MasterCard are developing an enforcement organization. They see the daily threat against their products. If credit card fraud continues to climb at the rates we are seeing, card usage, as we know it, could be at risk. Expect credit card companies to take action and retailers to be moved toward action.

Use All Three Principles to Leverage the Momentum Created by Compliance

While compliance itself does not create tremendous opportunity, the awareness it creates can help.

Corporate leaders are concerned with both company and personal liability. Again, this is an asset owner issue, not a custodial issue. Asset owners want to know what's hype and what's reality. Because you can provide real insight into core issues, you will have an audience. But don't focus on compliance itself; you will likely be delegated to some bureaucratic process. Focus on due care and the associated liability.

Then, using the concepts of ILM, ask questions to discover digital assets and learn about the liabilities associated with data loss.

Next, use policy to help companies limit liability while you help drive the architecture.

In the coming chapters, we will spend more time on how to leverage the concepts of threats and compliance, identify the asset owners and create high-impact messaging that will drive sales forward.

Summary

- ☑ Selling directly to a compliance committee is a long and difficult task.
- ☑ Moving the conversation toward due care reduces the seller's liability and allows customers' legal counsel to interpret which data is under consideration and how secure it must be.
- ☑ The seller's job becomes one of implementing controls that demonstrate due care.
- ☑ Get involved in policy. Compliance is driving many of today's policy changes, and it can reinforce or disqualify the products and services a firm recommends.
- ☑ Rather than selling technology to meet compliance, use the awareness of security from the growing number of regulations to reinforce the need to secure assets.

Chapter 5

Effective Boardroom Conversations

Convince buyers to rethink their security strategies and consider your products and services.

Learn to show data owners why their information is not as secure as they may think. If you can prove there's a problem, you can make the sale.

Several years ago, I worked for a company that was acquired by a global integrator.

During the transition, I seized the opportunity to create a national practice focusing on network and system security. It didn't take long to develop a business plan. The security market was growing, as were threats to the companies we solicited.

As a one-person security group, I wanted to work with our existing sales force to bring in midsize and large accounts. With my newly assigned quota in hand, I began calling salespeople nationwide to arrange meetings.

I was taken aback, however, when the salespeople I contacted each day responded with hesitation. They didn't view security as a priority and saw no need to set up a meeting. Nonetheless, I refused to give up.

I finally found a salesperson in South Carolina who was receptive to discussions.

Now, if you're familiar with South Carolina, you know there aren't many large accounts, with the exception of the I-85 Corridor.

Unfortunately, my new contact covered the eastern part of the state—far east of the accounts with which I was familiar. He happily announced he had a small firewall upgrade opportunity, with the possibility of converting the client to a brand we favored. I wasn't thrilled at the prospect of a four-hour drive for a potentially small deal.

Whenever a salesperson invites me to a meeting, my first question is always the same: "Are we meeting with an economic buyer?"

"Of course," the SC rep responded. "It's the IT director, who's also a vice president."

The buyer turned out to be a banker—and with three years of banking experience, I reminded the salesperson that virtually everyone who works at a bank is a vice president.

To avoid a long drive, I recommended a phone consultation. The call ended with the salesperson agreeing to arrange a meeting with a bank representative who had greater authority and purchasing power.

A few days later, I received a return call from the sales rep. He'd managed to arrange a meeting with an executive vice president. This sounded much more interesting to me, and so we set a date and I headed south.

I found myself seated in a meeting with three attendees from the customer side and the sales rep. The network administrator came to defend the bank's current firewall brand, the IT director was there to negotiate the deal, and the executive VP put in an appearance, but really didn't understand why he was needed at this technical meeting.

Must-Know Points for
Speaking with Asset Owners

In this chapter, we'll review the four key principles for communicating with executives and asset owners—the very principles, in fact, that made this sales call a success. I've used these concepts in many sales opportunities around the country and internationally.

Before I delineate the key points, let's examine the results of the bank meeting. It resulted in an agreement to perform a large risk assessment, which led to the following projects and product sales:

- Intrusion prevention appliances
- Email security appliance
- 24/7 security monitoring
- An investigation into a potential hacking incident
- Virtual private network (VPN)
- IP telephony implementation
- And, of course, a firewall sale, with a failover configuration and maintenance

In short, this meeting was a huge success. Let's explore how the sale was made.

Be Sure There's an Opportunity

Going into the meeting, I first needed to know an opportunity existed and where to find it. In the security arena, there's always an opportunity, as the sophistication of attacks increases. It's realistic to assume 90 percent of the companies you call on have inadequate security controls around a pivotal corporate asset: data.

You've probably watched other sales teams try (or have tried yourself) to convince a buyer to invest in security by pointing to the countless news reports of companies losing data, being hacked or suffering loss from an environmental outage. If you're like most salespeople, this approach has been unsuccessful. After 10 years of security news, prospects have become numb to the realities of security threats. After all, what's the likelihood they'll be attacked on the week you meet with them, when there's no evidence of malicious behavior?

This chapter will teach you how to show asset owners where threats really exist and why their current security architecture is inadequate. As I alluded to earlier, it involves four key principles, starting with three simple questions.

Establish a Foundation for Great Meetings

If we're going to convince buyers to move forward on security purchases or invest additional money on an infrastructure that includes security, we must prove their assets are at risk—that the impact and likelihood of an incident justifies moving forward.

As explained in Chapter 1, buyers will spend money on only four things: return on investment (ROI), operational efficiency, competitive advantage and risk mitigation—and security or risk mitigation leads the list. Other sales books may label these priorities differently, but whatever nomenclature you use, it boils down to the same concepts.

Four Things Economic Buyers Will Buy

ROI (Return on Investment) has been a strong argument for many technology organizations over the years. In 1972, Mack Hanan wrote the popular book *Consultative Selling,* which offers tremendous insights into using a database of norms/outcomes as customers buy one's products, allowing you to develop an ROI story. The problem with selling ROI in today's market, however, is the number of unqualified people who have tried to make a case for ROI. Buyers have become leery of this argument, calling for empirical data and case studies many of us are ill-equipped to present. If you have a strong financial background, you may be able to pull it off effectively, but the average salesperson breaks down when a CFO starts asking hard questions.

Operational efficiency can be a compelling argument. But when a 30-year-old stands in the office of a VP with 40 years of manufacturing experience, things can get rough. You may be asked: "And what do you know about management operations theory?"

Competitive-advantage arguments pose the same problem when we're dealing with organizations whose industries are foreign to us. Understanding vertical markets well enough to tell someone you're qualified to help him beat his competition takes courage and imagination.

Risk mitigation is altogether different, as we're dealing with technology that changes all the time. Understanding risk is relatively easy for those well versed in technology. A systems or network salesperson can get up to speed on information security without years of experience. In almost every sale, I lead with security; it doesn't matter what I'm selling.

Principles of Risk Management

The ability to manage risk is what data owners really want. As those ultimately liable in the event of a security breach, they need to make sure company data is protected from misuse or theft.

There are several key areas of risk management that I use to develop the security value proposition:

AAA: To the average product salesperson, AAA is just another three-letter acronym, treated almost as though it's a word. To the executive, it may be an automobile club. But in the sales call, it provides a structure for some very important questions.

1. Authentication: Identifying who's asking for data or network access—a critical area companies must control and maintain. Ask the data owner who should be accessing this information and how access is controlled.

2. Authorization: Providing users with different levels of access privileges, including what they are allowed to see, change, create, delete, etc. Find out who provides different levels of authorization privileges. How is this controlled with the data in question?

3. Accountability: The reporting mechanism that details who has access to specific information, who gave employees this access, when and what information was accessed, and what the employee did while accessing the data. Find out how this is done: Do they have a way to identify what users are doing?

MTD (Maximum Tolerable Downtime): A term often used in storage sales, but it's really a security question: How much downtime can you afford? The asset owner's answer likely differs from the custodian's. Find out how important data is and how long the company can survive if it's unavailable. This speaks to the impact of loss of availability.

RPO (Restore Point Objective): Another storage term that focuses on how much data loss is acceptable. At what point must you be able to restore, and how much data can be lost between a backup and system failure? Again, this question focuses on the impact of data loss.

CIA (Confidentiality, Integrity and Availability): Often considered the three pillars of security, each should be considered with the asset owner. Most of us think only of confidentiality or privacy of data, but the integrity and availability requirements are equally important.

Each of these topics is used to build a picture of risk in the mind of the buyer. Risk is simply a look at impact versus likelihood (see illustration, right).

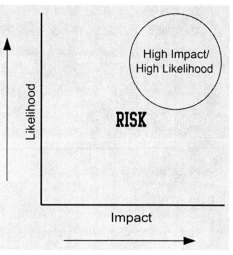

The concepts delineated in the figure provide a framework for asking questions that uncover key assets, as well as the impact associated with losing confidentiality, availability, data integrity, etc. If the impact is high, the issue is worth considering. The question is, what is the likelihood?

When a plane goes down, the impact is always high. The question risk managers start asking center around the likelihood of whether this will happen again. What is the likelihood that a plane will be sitting on the runway that's too short, while air traffic control is staffed by only one person who's not paying attention and gives the go-ahead to take off? The pilots, unfamiliar with the airport, push their throttles forward and accelerate down the runway, only to find the strip is too short. You may remember an incident like this from 2006, and a tragedy resulted. So, what is the likelihood it will happen again? Is it high enough for someone to do something about it?

As a salesperson, you have little ability to change impact; however, you can change likelihood. Your sales call should focus on likelihood, looking for the safeguards that may be used to reduce the likelihood of data being compromised.

If you have ever tried to sell denial-of-service (DDOS) products, you know what I'm talking about. Few sales have been closed around these products, unless the buyer has experienced a DDOS in the past. While the impact may be high, the likelihood is not high enough to justify the sale.

Layers of Security

When selling a security strategy, the concept of security layers that work together to protect assets allows you to create a vision. As you will see in later chapters, it doesn't make sense to sell a security product by itself, unless you're simply completing another provider's security strategy. Three types of controls must be considered:

1. Technical controls: traditional security controls like firewalls, intrusion detection software, passwords. Most companies will have at least a firewall in place and perhaps VPN technology. More are implementing intrusion detection/protection software and appliances this year, but they alone will not protect data.

2. Physical controls: Examples include controlled access to wiring closets/data centers where devices can be compromised, security cameras or even security guards positioned in the lobby. Your client will frequently have some form of protection, but will lack the security controls necessary to keep users from accessing ports on computers in public-access locations.

All three layers are required to build a sound security architecture. Most companies haven't thought them through in a consistent manner.

3. Administrative controls: These are almost always inadequate. Security policies, disaster recovery and business continuity plans, and security and event correlation reports fall into this category. Companies usually lacking well-written, tested plans, and policies are seldom maintained or enforced.

The Four Key Principles for Communicating with Data Owners

"You get delegated to those you sound like," writes sales expert Michael Bosworth. Remember this quote every time you walk into a decision maker's office. Then, when you're redirected to the IT group, admit you must have sounded like an IT person: way too technical. If you're going to sell security, a more business-centric dialogue has to evolve for nontechnical meetings composed of less presentation and more conversation.

In my SC sales call, I had a decision to make: How do I keep the meeting focused on the asset owner? With the technical person and decision maker both in the room, we somehow need to keep the meeting interesting to that executive. Once a technical line of discussion begins to dominate, the executive leaves—something we've all experienced. I use the four principles in the illustration on page 63 to connect directly with the buyer.

Principle #1: Ask the Three Questions

When selling security, you must have access to data owners with liability. But what are you going to talk about if you can't discuss products? In every sales call, I use the same outline, modifying the three questions based on the situation. The SC meeting was no exception. Turning to the buyer, I asked these three questions:

> **Question 1:** What are you trying to protect?
> **Question 2:** What are the relevant threats?
> **Question 3:** How comfortable are you with your organization's ability to detect, and respond to, a recognized threat before data is compromised?

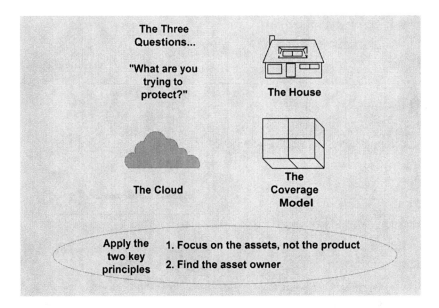

The Three Questions...

"What are you trying to protect?"

The House

The Cloud

The Coverage Model

Apply the two key principles
1. Focus on the assets, not the product
2. Find the asset owner

Question 1

Your first objective: Steer away from a product meeting and focus on assets. The first question allows you to achieve this by concentrating on your prospect's mission-critical data by simply asking him to identify it.

Again, the person you must speak with is the data owner. You're not looking for the security administrator's opinion. You want to know the data owner's position on where risk exists.

There are a number of acceptable answers, but "the network" isn't one of them. You're looking for data that exposes the owner to liability or places the company's reputation as a secure institution in jeopardy. When I ask this question, I explain I'm looking for the items that would greatly impact the business if compromised or inaccessible. If the question is framed correctly, I expect dialogue on mission-critical systems.

In my SC meeting, we spent the first 20 minutes of our meeting on this first question.

At the end of our dialogue, I had a thorough understanding of the client's key assets and the impact associated with loss or compromise. I had the bottom line of my risk graph (right).

Question 2

Next, I must determine the likely threats. The data owner may not be aware of all impending security threats. Finding out what he believes is real—and most risky to his company—is helpful in developing a business case for security.

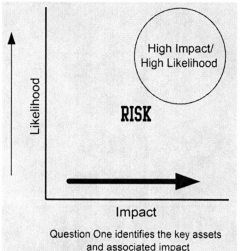

Question One identifies the key assets and associated impact

Also ask if he's laying off IT people, has challenges with other internal staff, uses various contractors or is open to other guest users. This is a good time to uncover any past security issues.

In my SC meeting, we spent another 10–15 minutes on this topic, but at the end I had a clear understanding of the likely threats he anticipated. I had part of the Y axis of my risk graph (above).

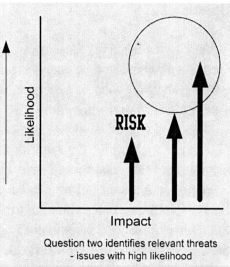

Question two identifies relevant threats - issues with high likelihood

Question 3

The final question is a quick one. Determining the prospect's comfort level with his current security strategy will tell you a great deal about how well he understands today's security threats. It completes my risk graph by giving me a picture of how likely the data owner believes these threats may be.

If, for example, the prospect is very comfortable, you know you have to do some educating. The FBI, CIA, other government entities and many major U.S. banks have been hacked successfully in the last few years. It's hard to believe anyone would feel "very" comfortable at this time.

In most cases, I expect buyers to indicate some level of ignorance about the true state of their ability to defend their assets. They likely fail to see any real evidence of danger; however, at some point they may report a security breach.

By the time you've asked the third question, you should have a clear understanding of your buyers' key assets, top threats (the ones they know about), priority of systems and comfort level. You have the entire risk graph built.

At this point, you must provide a compelling reason to consider changes in the organization's approach to security. I do this by explaining how security works and why their systems are likely less secure than they think.

Let me reiterate: These three questions are designed to shift the focus from products to assets. Technical security influencers then no longer need to defend their current product choices.

> **The three questions: Stop focusing on product, and focus on assets—what are you trying to protect.**

Principle #2: Show Buyers How to Think About Security

The three questions will consume most of your meeting time. They allow you to build the risk graph, providing a clear picture of where the opportunity exists. Your next goal: Show buyers how any security architecture must operate. I want them to see that most companies, including theirs, have likely approached this topic inadequately. I use the analogy of a house: a physical structure we like to consider safe.

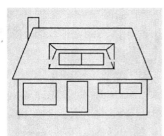

The House

After drawing a simple house on a whiteboard, I ask the buyer to share how he secures his house. During this brainstorming exercise, he'll usually call out measures like "doors," "windows," "locks," "gun," "dog," "alarm" and the like. We then have a simple chart that looks something like the chart below.

Doors	Alarm	Dog
Locks	Motion detector	Gun
Windows	Monitoring	Police
Fence	Crime watch	Insurance

I then divide this list into three columns, asking the buyer to help me categorize his lists. Notice that I've grouped the items in a particular order, regardless of how they were given to me.

1.	2.	3.
Doors	Alarm	Dog
Locks	Motion detector	Gun
Windows	Monitoring	Police
Fence	Crime watch	Insurance

What criteria are used for each list? Businesspeople usually guess that the first list applies to a home's physical features; however, they are all physical. I refer to Column 1 as my proactive protection column. Once Column 1 is labeled, it is easy to conclude that the second column is about detection, while Column 3 applies to response. It's my PDR Model: protection, detection, response. Every security architecture in the world (that works) is based on these three pillars.

It's now time to ask this important question: "Which column is most critical to security?"

Most asset owners choose Column 1: protection. They believe keeping things out is always best. While this is theoretically true, security architecture has always relied more on Column 2 to secure assets. Here's why: We were sitting in a bank, and I asked my client if his doors were open. He replied yes. I then asked if his vault was open; again, he responded with a nod.

"So, what is protecting the money?" I asked. There are many layers of security in a bank. Cameras and security guards observe activity throughout the day. If someone violates policy, steps behind the teller line, draws a weapon or wanders down the wrong hallway, a well-timed response plan will kick in. And how about at night? The doors are locked, but could easily be broken through if crooks don't care about the threat of the alarm system.

Our bodies operate on this principle. While we have skin and clothing to protect us, we come in contact each day with bacteria that are detected and killed by our immune system. If we lacked an immune system, our skin and clothing would be ineffective against attack.

One's house, too, has no real security without detection. The idea that your doors or windows will deter a determined intruder is clearly wrong thinking.

Again, the point of these comparisons is to draw our buyer into a clear example he's very familiar with—to show him there are three critical aspects to security architecture and that the detection process is vital to asset protection.

Principle# 3: Show How Easily You Can Break In

Once the buyer sees that detection is the most important area to focus on, it's now time to illustrate how easily one can infiltrate a company's network.

I like to draw a simple two-cloud network, showing the internal network and the Internet; then, I quickly demonstrate how a bot network (botnet) is established (see illustration, next page).

You can use the following example: People love to receive

email. And no matter how many times they're told, "Don't open that email," they continue to do it. There are many roads into a network, including email, instant messaging (IM), Really Simple Syndication (RSS) and compromised websites.

The most basic music, video and picture downloads can be used to infect systems. Certainly, more than half the spam out there is infected. If I were an attacker, all I would need to do is convince the recipient to click on a link or open a file, allowing me to install malware on a system. And all I need for access is one computer out of the hundreds or thousands a company might own.

It is easy to break in. Anyone who really wants to can.

In our threat chapter, we reviewed how this is done, so without providing all of the technical details, I illustrate how I can bypass firewalls and take over. The point is, firewalls don't stop many of the threats used by organized crime in this information-theft era.

Next comes a key question—the point where you expose weaknesses in your prospect's security architecture. Turning back to the house model, I ask: "Which column does your company rely upon most to protect your digital assets?"

The answer is predictable. The company may have some intrusion prevention software running at the perimeter, but the ability to detect and respond to attacks throughout the computing environment is generally quite weak. Most of your customers will be unable to detect and respond to attacks coming from wireless networks, remote access, compromised laptops, Bluetooth technology and the like.

When this process is handled correctly, the data owner will

realize his security strategy was built around an approach that sounded good 10 years ago: the idea that a firewall would protect the internal network from Internet threats and that a password would do the rest. At this point, without debating with the technical team, you've brought your buyer to a new understanding of how risk is reduced.

You may ask at this point, "What if the buyer doesn't agree"? Take him back to Column 1 of the house model. What would you have to do to secure the house through Column 1? Some military facilities rely heavily on Column 1, yet those in charge understand it's not enough. With a house, you'd need to spend hundreds of thousands of dollars—and even into the millions—to create a perfectly safe home without relying on detection schemes – and still it wouldn't really work. Does the buyer really want to build a castle with insurmountable walls, moats and razor wire? It's completely "over the top" and unnecessary when you realize it costs about $30 a month to hire a security monitoring company, with alarm equipment included. It becomes clear, with proper analysis, that detection response is a key part of any security strategy—and your prospect's security architecture likely lacks this type of strategy.

Principle #4: Demonstrate Holistic Security

Explaining the holistic security approach is the final step in your meeting. I call this table "The Coverage Model." It gives the data owner a better understanding of how the right security will defend corporate assets.

	P	D	R
Admin	Policy		BCP/DR
Tech		IDS	
Physical		Check badges	Guards

I use a simple three-by-three grid, taking the concepts from the house illustration—protection, detection and response—and combining them with three basic types of security controls (administrative, technical, and physical). Don't fill in the entire table; instead, quickly illustrate how these nine boxes provide a comprehensive approach to securing data. Most companies focus on these boxes as silos or spend the majority of their time working on just one or two. Data owners really need to view these as integrated controls that work together through the infrastructure and organization to enable a strong security architecture.

Using this diagram, I looked at a decision maker in SC and said: "It's not the firewall we should be talking about. As you can see, these issues have little to do with firewalls and brute-force hacking." Security is not a firewall conversation; it's a matter of assets and risk, the likely threats and their ultimate impact.

My response: "No, I guarantee they will break in. The question is, will you be able to detect and respond before your assets are compromised?"

The buyer may, at this point, ask whether security will prevent hackers from breaking in and stealing his data. My response: "No, I guarantee they will break in. The question is, will you be able to detect and respond before your assets are compromised?"

Bringing These Four Principles Together

Now, I am not suggesting that you draw this house in every sales call; however, the house works. People have said, "I don't think I could draw that simple picture for a CIO of a major corporation."

Well, I have.

I have used it in board meetings, executive-level association meetings, keynotes, sales calls informal dinners and when talking with businesspeople. They respond, "You are the first person who has been able to explain this complex topic in terms I can really understand."

But it's not the house that matters; it's the key principles:

1. The three questions move the meeting away from product and onto the assets. You can do this any way you want, but somehow you must set the foundation for the meeting at the executive level—and on the assets.

2. The House: However you want to do it, you must show the buyer what security really is and get him to admit he doesn't have it.

3. The Cloud: Asset owners need to see how easy it is to break in and that the firewall team doesn't really understand this.

4. The Coverage Model: Finally, they need to see that this is not a product issue that should be delegated to the IT organization. Asset protection requires holistic thinking around products, policies, procedures, education, etc. It's a big issue, and they need someone who really understands it.

Security Sinkholes

In my security-sales workshops, attendees frequently ask, "What if prospects have everything they need—or say they have it all covered?" It's a great question—and it will happen.

First, if you're talking to a data owner or other senior management, he generally won't assert he has everything covered. The most common response tends to be: "I'm not sure we have what we need. What do you recommend?"

For the company that has done everything reasonable to secure its data, I whip out my trusty security sinkhole list—a compilation of the areas almost always lacking in due care:

• Compliance

- Policy and liability
- Perimeter
- Wi-Fi
- Identity management
- Remote access
- Information life-cycle
- Applications
- BCP/DR
- Messaging
- Mobility/connectivity
- The "People Factor"

In particular, areas like remote access, wireless, user awareness and application security are severely lacking. The perimeter may have most of what's needed, but when we start moving to these other areas, I find networks and systems to be very insecure.

With this in mind, I remind the data owner that more than 300 major organizations reported losing identity information in the last twelve months, exposing more than 100 million people to identity theft.

It would be foolish for someone to feel completely secure, given the news we read every day.

If my audience is more technically inclined or refuses to admit any weaknesses, I congratulate them on being ahead of the curve. I then continue my marketing efforts in other areas of the organization or begin reaching out to other prospects. There is no value in debating individuals who won't admit their weaknesses or remain loyal to another security provider.

The table beginning on the next page lists some of the major areas where security opportunities can be found in today's IS/IT landscape.

Remember: We are focusing on the business processes as we consider technology areas in this table. The affected business process is where the risk will be measured and the value proposition will be developed.

Security Sinkhole	Notes and Opportunities
Compliance	**Business Use:** Both federal and private security standards are required in many businesses. Visa CISP, HIPAA, GLBA, SOX and Basel II are all examples of current regulations with tremendous opportunity. **Opportunity Idea:** • All companies want to know how much risk they have. • Some companies may incur fines or be subject to arrest if not compliant. Learn how you can help them.
Perimeter architecture	**Business Use:** Internet, extranet, remote access and web-accessible applications are critical to most businesses today. All depend on a secure perimeter architecture. Most companies have problems. **Opportunity Idea:** • Assess outside connectivity requirements and secure based on need. • Replace IPSec architectures with newer SSL technologies. • Improve security through detection and correlation technologies. • Extend perimeter through endpoint security technologies. • Provide security monitoring to detect attacks before data is stolen.
Wi-Fi	**Business Use:** Most businesses are starting to use Wi-Fi for traveling employees, mobility in-house, guest access and less costly network implementations at remote facilities. **Opportunity Idea:** • Assess security and remediate • Provide strong authentication controls. • Add endpoint security controls and centralized management.

Identity management	**Business Use:** Provisioning, password management, accountability and reporting are all critical to the liability and compliance aspects of security, and they are generally out of control.
	Opportunity Idea: • Create centralized policy-based management. • Centralize provisioning and password management. • Consolidate identity data. • Introduce single sign-on solutions.
Remote access and endpoint security	**Business Use:** Almost all companies have end-users who travel or work from home. Business depends on it.
	Opportunity Idea: • Endpoint security controls-policy based • Access control improvements • Event monitoring and reporting
Information life-cycle management	**Business Use:** At each stage of the business process, information is created, used, transmitted and stored. Eventually, it is deleted or archived. Each stage has inherent risks that must be dealt with.
	Opportunity Idea: • Create policies that govern classification. • Provide secure archival and document management. • Define and train the company on data disposal.
Applications (web and back-end processing)	**Business Use:** Web applications frequently front-end major business applications. Most in-house, and many purchased web applications have major security holes.
	Opportunity Idea: • Conduct application security testing. • Address security coding. • Add security controls to applications.

DR/BCP	**Business Use:** All hardware and many applications will fail at some point. Every major business process should be assessed for risk levels and addressed for business continuity and disaster recovery.
	Opportunity Idea: • Perform business impact analysis. • Introduce high-availability computing. • Work with clients on planning. • Provide co-location services.
Messaging	**Business Use:** If computers are used, the company is likely using email and instant messaging. Email is insecure, and all messaging applications invite security threats.
	Opportunity Idea: • Help companies defend against malware. • Secure archival and retrieval products. • Policies that govern transmission, deletion, archival, etc. • Content inspection controls
Mobility and universal connectivity	**Business Use:** Everything is connected today and must support a diverse business climate. Mobility and connectivity introduce many security issues.
	Opportunity Idea: • Defense against botcode and other malware attacks • Access control and strong authentication, provisioning, etc. • Secure transmission controls • Monitoring for malicious activity • Remote device security (such as encryption)
End users and IT personnel	**Business Use:** Users/IT personnel make mistakes.
	Opportunity Idea: • Provide security education services • Assess risk and provide managed services to create a separation of duty. • Introduce policy enforcement controls.

When to Involve the Security Team

Finally, one last question always comes up: "When do I get the security teams involved, and do we continue to align our security team with the client's security team?" It's another great question.

Remember, bringing their security people too early is an immediate demotion from the asset owner to the IT/ security organization—an introduction you don't yet want. In the coming chapters, we will address a sequence of events to help guide you through the selling process. This information provides you with the key principles for communicating with executives and asset owners: the people with liability.

Remember: Security is sold to asset owners, approved by IT decision makers and implemented by security consultants from your organization. It can then be managed and maintained by your team or an internal security team. Selling to the security team is likely the biggest time waster when trying to close business.

Summary

- ☑ Use the three questions from this chapter to move the sales meeting from product to assets. Refuse to get into a product discussion at this point in the sales process.
- ☑ Use the house or a similar illustration to show data owners that security requires a balance of protection, detection and response.
- ☑ Get the buyer to see he's likely over-relying on protection.
- ☑ Illustrate how easy it is to break into most companies with bots and other malware, showing buyers the importance of critical detection.
- ☑ Use the coverage model to demonstrate how a holistic security approach works.
- ☑ Point out security sinkholes that will be the weak links in your prospect's security architecture.

Chapter 6

Effective Value Propositions

How do you build an effective value proposition for executives?

You have only a few seconds to turn short introductions or first-time meetings into strategic relationships. Security provides a perfect place to start.

Having an effective message may be the most important concept in this book. A friend always asks me, "What common task must you do uncommonly well if you are to succeed in business?"

He then offers the example of a surgeon. Picture a surgeon—someone who has trained for years to perform complex operations on your heart or another critical organ. You need surgery, so you look for the physician who seems best qualified. You find one who you think can do the job. His resume is outstanding, he's performed this procedure many times, and every operation has been a success.

The surgeon agrees to perform the operation and begins the work. He spends hours meticulously working to get every aspect of the operation just right, and finally he has solved the problem. He sews up the incisions and, as he's leaving the OR, it suddenly occurs to him that he forgot to wash his hands.

Our family has spent many years building successful businesses. My father was an early entrepreneur. Throughout my childhood, I had the opportunity to watch him build his business. My brother-in-law has been doing the same for more than 20 years, and I have followed this path, working in several technology startups, as well as my current consulting practice. Continuing the legacy, I have involved my children in building businesses as part of their education. My daughters have sewn clothes, cleaned houses and baked cookies. Some of my children have raised bees and sold honey, and my oldest son has developed a small business, building a specialized exercise platform he distributes through physical therapy offices.

The other day, my son came to me, looking for ideas on how to expand his exercise-platform business. We talked about advertising, phonebook ads, signs and even reaching out to neighbors or cold calling.

I reminded him that his product sells primarily when a physical therapist recommends it to a patient. Not many people would really understand its value if he were to put up signs. But for some reason, when a doctor or physical therapist recommends something, we will pay hundreds of dollars for a simple piece of plastic that sits in our shoe or for a pulley that hangs on a door to stretch a repaired rotator cuff. Somewhat disappointed, my son went on his way.

The next day, he came back to me, excited about a recent sale to a woman who exercises in our neighborhood. When I asked how he made the sale, he told me she walks down our road each day, so he decided to stop and talk to her about stretching before exercising, explaining how it would help. After a few minutes, she agreed to buy a platform.

What is my son's value proposition? It's simple: He's 11. It's hard for people to turn down a young boy as he's building his own business.

Unfortunately, you and I aren't that cute. We have to come up with something that grabs the attention of adults who are too busy to stop and build a relationship with everyone they meet.

The Error of Having No Value Proposition

Let's take a real-world technology example. Several years ago, I served as vice president of a mid-size solution provider. I was responsible for bottom-line profitability.

One day, while sitting in my office, my administrative assistant paged me, asking if I would join Bob, our sales manager, in the conference room. He needed my help ASAP.

When I arrived, I immediately saw the problem. Bob was sitting across the table from an engineer from a company that manufactures routers and switches. We already had a partnership with one of the largest providers of network technology, and this engineer was working hard to convince Bob that his technology was superior. With very limited network experience, Bob sat with a glazed look on his face. As I sat down, I noticed two other men in the room dressed in suits.

I let them go on for about five minutes before interrupting the engineer to reintroduce everyone. I quickly learned that we had a local channel manager, regional manager and the speaker, an engineer from South Carolina.

Once introduced, the engineer started again, but I quickly interrupted him. Looking over at the regional manager, I had one simple question: "How are we going to make more money in the coming year if we take on this product"? The regional manager looked over at the engineer and began to explain that his company's superior technology was a sure winner and asked that we continue to technical overview.

Looking again at the manager I said, "Well, that isn't really what I'm asking. I want to know how I'm going to make more incremental income if we take on the product." He was taken aback by the question, not understanding why the technology didn't interest me. I explained that we were selling a lot of our current partner's product, and I didn't really understand how this product would turn into more money.

He didn't have an answer for me. At that point, I thought it was best to end the meeting and have them go back to their office and find an answer. I promised I would make time to meet again when they had one. It's been almost nine years since they left my office, and I still haven't heard back from them. I'm starting to think they may never call back. Actually, I think they failed to develop a value proposition that mattered to the economic buyer.

The Importance of a Value Proposition

If you're like most people, you meet new contacts every day. It may be in a large enterprise account, across several mid-sized accounts or among many smaller accounts. You see them at trade shows, marketing events, association meetings, in hallways and in meetings you attend. But what happens to them? Chances are most of them never turn into anything more than a one-time contact.

If you learn one thing from this book, it should be the importance of building effective messaging. When I work with resellers in security or sales workshops, I ask them to write down what they tell people when they're introduced or when answering the question, "What do you do"? If you work for a manufacturer, at least you have a brand. But as a solution provider, you really have nothing outside the intellectual capital you and your teams possess to solve business problems. Creating differentiation is the key. Let's look at what some of these people care about.

IT Personnel

When I refer to IT personnel, I'm not talking about CIOs, but the average IT office workers—people who oversee networks and systems every day. In my workshops, we usually have quite a bit of dialogue about what the IT person really cares about.

If you've never worked on this side of the business, you may be in for a shock. It's not about time, saving money or beating the competition through technology. Sure, there are exceptions to the rule, but of the many people who have come up the ranks from that side of the business (as well as the teams I've managed and worked with in pharmaceuticals and banking), it seems the average IT worker is most concerned with the following: compensation, having a great manager, having less work to do, getting into the right cubicle, free lunches, golf outings and, perhaps most important, access to cool technology.

With technology, we're not talking about the mission-critical systems, but the new high-tech offerings and access to smart technical people that allow IT people to learn and enhance their resumes. And if they could somehow reach the part of their career where they have their own CAN—(cubicle area network); you know, with the best desktop system and most memory and disk space—this is real status. Having their own printer, file server, router or other cool technology right in their own cubicle is the dream of every custodian.

So, why do we spend so much time negotiating with, and writing detailed proposals with pricing, for these people? The negotiation process you've been going through with these people is really a front for getting the things that are important to IT. In the end, the percent-off doesn't matter; this person has no budget.

Learn how you can help IT people become successful, and you will win the trust and friendship you're looking for—if you can deliver it. But don't mistake them for the buyer.

Department Managers

Unlike IT people, managers on the profit-center side of the business have budgets and financial goals that earn them bonuses and reputation. This is where you often find buyers who are also early adopters of technology. If they can find new technology that puts them ahead of the competition, they are likely to buy it.

Department managers also jockey for positions, but it has more to do with building a strategic profit center than with knowing about cool technology.

CXO Executives

There may be various terms or descriptions used for this job title, but the bottom line is shareholder value. This is true primarily for CEOs, whereas CIOs might see more incentive around uptime. CSOs do not really fit into this category.

CSO/CISO

This may sound like two different titles, but across companies there is no consistency. When you visit various companies and analyze what these people do, there's no clear, consistent distinction across organizations. Some companies have a CSO, others a CISO, and some have both. In some cases, we see one reporting to the other, or vice versa. What's truly important are the many regulations that require a C-level security officer, which is why companies hire them.

CSO/CISOs may come from big accounting firms, consulting firms or IT. In most cases, the position is ill defined and carries limited decision-making power when it comes to technology choices; however, in most cases, you need a checkmark from this person. Selling secure solutions against the recommendations of the CSO is an uphill battle. But this is not the place to start when selling security.

Each of these positions requires a slightly different message. As you build your value proposition, keep in mind who you're talking to and what their personal goals and responsibilities dictate.

A Simple Definition of "Trusted Advisor"

"Trusted advisor" may be an overused term—one that has lost its original meaning as sales organizations use it to refer to just about every relationship they have. Somehow, companies have embraced the idea they can go out and be a customer's trusted advisor without really trying.

But the trusted advisor role really is critical. The economic buyer, the person who can say "yes" when others have said "no," relies on this individual. As the name implies, the trusted advisor must be trustworthy and capable of advising. This seems simple—perhaps even silly when you first read it. The "trusted" part of the phrase should be a given, but many salespeople are not trustworthy.

What about the concept of "advisor"? Do you have knowledge a client would value, for which he'd be willing to pay? Think for a moment of all the salespeople who have called on you in the last few years. Were they able to "advise" you? If you're going to move into this highly regarded position, you must have some intellectual capital that matters to clients. If you simply sell storage, networks, servers or other hardware and software products, chances are you have nothing on which to advise your clients. Perhaps your only value at this point is to supply products at reasonable prices—not a long-term position of strength.

"I believe that 30% of the technology sales force will go away over the next 5 years," Mack Hanan, author of *Consultative Selling*, told me at a recent dinner meeting. His comments come from watching the commoditization of technology hardware and executives who can operate without advice when it comes to building networks, installing servers and bringing in basic infrastructure. As companies continue to make it easier to implement these technologies, more sales will be conducted over the Internet, with the IT department limited to installing it.

But this doesn't mean there will be no place for technology consultants. There are still many areas where advice and direction

83

are needed. The question is, are you ready to advise? When I conduct security workshops, salespeople frequently comment, "I don't want to become a security expert; I have consultants who do that." The problem with this attitude is that salespeople are still under the impression they can build relationships with executives just by being a great person. Because everyone works under this assumption, there is a need for differentiation. One manufacturer I worked with has thousands of direct salespeople in the United States, plus more than 8,000 partner resellers. Something has to be different if you are going to reach the buyers.

The Key to Becoming a Trusted Advisor

A friend from the National Speakers Association (NSA) recently shared a story about how he remained in an advisory capacity. It doesn't take much to be the expert in an area like security. Art was part of a safety organization within a transportation company. He eventually left to become a professional speaker. At first, it was hard to find work, but one of his colleagues encouraged him to become more of an advisor and to focus on the area of safety (part of the security world, but not digital).

Looking for ways to accomplish this, Art began to study what I call "sound bites." He took the most pressing issues and frequently asked questions and began studying and memorizing sound-bite answers. Soon, Art's name was getting out, and he was being interviewed on radio programs, speaking at events and being asked for advice. Over the next few years, he became one of the most highly paid safety-focused speakers in the NSA.

Art's story isn't unique. I've heard similar tales from others, and I've done it myself, using sound bites that come from security trade magazines like *SC Magazine* (worth subscribing to at scmagazine.com; free to those who sell in this industry). Publications like this are full of management-level sound bites on data theft, cyber-crime, malware and product announcements. If you read a monthly magazine like this for 30 minutes, you will sound like an expert—and that is all you need. You get 30 minutes with the asset owner, sell him on the concepts presented here and introduce your technical people to his when it's time. As an example, I have listed several sound bites I have used over the past year, some of which I have already cited in this book.

List of Sound-Bite Examples

• Microsoft estimates 60 percent of all PCs outside the corporation are infected with a remote-control agent (bot).

• Microsoft estimates an average of 6 percent of all systems within the corporation are controlled by a bot—and you only need one to have data stolen.

• SC Magazine estimates 250,000 new systems become zombies each day.

• Denial-of-service attacks have increased by 400 percent in the last year, according to SC Magazine.

• More than 60 percent of all hacks involve an insider, notes Cybertrust.

• The average publicly held company loses about 10 percent of its shareholder value when identities are compromised. It takes about a year to recover. (Source: CIO magazine)

• It costs a company an average of $600,000 to notify customers when their identities are stolen.

The key point here: Clients will choose advisors based on what they need to know to be successful. The advisor will be invited to planning meetings, have insights into where the organization is going and will be the one consulted when decisions are made.

The relevance to security is this: Data owners need help in making sure their assets are safe. They won't go to their own IT people, so they need someone from the outside who they can trust. That person needs to be you, which moves you from a vendor to an advisor.

The things that will help you become a trusted advisor may include your industry knowledge in a vertical market like healthcare, references that show you've been successful at providing security to similar organizations, product knowledge and integration ability, awareness of what's happening in the security market, knowledge of the cyber-crime world, etc.

Clients will ultimately choose their trusted advisors. Will you be one of them?

Two Components of the Value Proposition

You meet people every day. What happens to them? In the last 12 months, I've added about 500 names to my database, but can I phone these people next week and get them to take my call? Will they remember who I am? Are they willing to meet with me if I do call?

In my coaching practice, I frequently ask salespeople who they're meeting and whether these relationships have been built versus being mere acquaintances. In most cases, the latter is true. How can you begin to change this trend and start turning introductions into meaningful relationships?

The Problem with your Elevator Pitch

Most of us have been given an elevator pitch—something developed by our marketing group to explain what we do in a few seconds. The pitch has to be quick enough to share in an elevator—high impact, but to the point.

The problem with most elevator pitches is they're all about us. A salesperson will say, "Let me tell you how great I am so you can buy something from me."

One day, I was in an elevator with the president and CEO of a nationwide bank I worked for. I'd just had my review, and while my marks were excellent, I was somewhat disappointed with my title and income level. There we were, just the two of us, and I thought to myself, "What can I say to get this person to see my value?" I couldn't come up with anything meaningful. Now, looking back, I realize why. Anything I said would have sounded like a sales pitch. The CEO would have likely seen it as a cheap attempt to point out my greatness, and he would have quickly dismissed it as a character flaw.

In my workshops, I tell salespeople that the elevator pitch can be compared to throwing up on someone. It doesn't feel good, and it doesn't have a positive outcome. It is usually filled with esoteric language, industry vernacular and meaningless marketing-created terms.

Understanding the Value Proposition

The value proposition is different. It's an introduction that gives someone an understanding of what you can do for him. It's focused on his needs—a brief description of the benefits you can bring. It's not a list of features, so if you're going to provide this benefit statement, it's essential to have some idea of what the potential client needs before you start talking.

The value proposition is a valuable way to share your worth with a client, but he has to be ready to hear it. He has to ask for it. This is the key: getting the prospect or client to ask you for your value.

Two Essential Parts of the Value Proposition

I like to break messaging into two parts. First comes the advisory positioning statement (what I call the APS), a quick way to position myself with a potential client. It must be short enough to be an introduction, yet provide sufficient content to grab the person's interest. It must push him to ask the question, "What is your value proposition?" By doing this, I gain the listener's attention, which in turn creates an opportunity for me to deliver an effective value proposition.

The Advisory Positioning Statement

The advisory positioning statement is my introduction. I use it in hallways, at meetings where I have just a moment to speak, or when meeting someone at an association event or conference. It's the short one-minute introduction that allows me to grab his attention.

If you look at most introductions, you will likely agree they don't actually amount to anything. You are introduced to someone's coworker, colleague or manager, and you introduce yourself as a salesperson or consultant. If you are thinking, you ask for a card. But from there, it's all chance. You might follow up with an email, or you might even place a call if you are really proactive. But in most cases, nothing happens. So, how do you turn this around and make it something more strategic?

If you've ever been to North Carolina, you know there is a lot of clay. It's nearly impossible to grow grass without spending a lot of time and money. If you were to look over my yard, it's like looking over a desert. The clay soil is hard and barren, with big weeds sprouting from crevasses that form from the intense heat, and then there are huge mounds of fire-ant hills. Each year, I plant grass, it rains, the seeds wash into the woods, and I am left with what looks like a scene from an Arizona desert.

A few weeks ago, I received a note in the mail that advertised a lawn-care service that would come to my property and analyze my grass. It was a free assessment. I thought this would be a great way to get some answers.

When the person arrived, he began to look over my yard. Once the assessment was complete, he came to the door to deliver the bad news.

Before letting Scott, our local grass specialist, begin, I asked him about his value proposition. I clearly caught him off guard with this question, but he finally responded with several comments, such as "industry leader in lawn care, better customer service, greener lawns" and the like.

"Scott, that is a terrible value proposition," I replied. "What benefit is there in this statement that really means something to me?"

Looking at my yard, I placed my hand on Scott's shoulder and said, "Scott, look at my lawn. You know how hard it is to grow grass in North Carolina,"?

"Yes, we have a program to fix this," he said.

"Scott, that is your value proposition," I informed him. "If you had come to me and said, 'Dave, you know how hard it is to grow grass out here in this heat?' I would have said, 'Yes, look at my yard.'"

Scott could have empathized with me, saying "I see the problem. There is a simple solution. I specialize in fixing this problem!" And I would have replied, "Scott, tell me—what do I do?"

You know how hard it is for companies to know who is accessing specific data at any given time?

You know how difficult it is for middle- market managers to focus on their business and still give time to IT?

You know hard it is to make sure that every system that connects to a company's network—whether a laptop, remote user, partner, third-party consultant or customer—is who they say they are, and aren't doing anything they're unauthorized to do?

You know how hard it is to detect someone doing something he shouldn't be doing, and to stop him before he damages or steals something?

If you could come up with a simple question that starts with "You know how…"—one that resonates with the person you are meeting and causes him to say, "Yeah, that's a problem. We struggle with that all the time"—we would have an opportunity to say, "This is what I focus on. There is a solution."

This prompts the client to ask for the program or process developed to fix the problem—a unique, yet affordable, process. It gets him to ask you for your value proposition. And once I asked about the program, Scott was in a position to share his value proposition, with my undivided attention.

Using My APS

In late 2006, I had the opportunity to meet a channel executive from a large software company. My contact, a channel manager in the mid-Atlantic, asked me if I'd like to meet his manager. I was excited about the opportunity, but he then told me the meeting would take place at a trade show—a forum of thousands of custodians milling around, hunting for free T-shirts and pens. I would have to buy my own ticket and spend the day traveling for a short meeting amid chaos. Was this a good opportunity?

I took the chance, thinking this is my only opportunity. When I arrived, it was lunchtime and, as I had predicted, we were surrounded by noise and confusion. My contact brought me to the restaurant where his manager was eating with a group of people, another obstacle to any meeting with a purpose. But look at what happened next.

I extended my welcome to the East Coast channel manager, leading with my name, followed by my APS. (You know how difficult it is to get your resellers to understand the value message of your organization? They seem to focus on the commodity products, leaving out the most important aspects of your program.)

Jim' s eyes lit up. He said, "Yes, that is the problem."

"That is what I focus on," I quickly replied.

"Really!" he said. "Tell me what you do."

I told him I'd show him, but we would need to set up a short meeting at his office to go over it. We arranged the meeting, but it didn't end there.

In the follow-up meeting, he called his manager (the U.S. channel manager) and asked him to meet with me. We set the meeting for a few weeks later.

As I sat down in his office, his first question was: "Dave, what is your value proposition?"

I almost fell out of my chair when I heard those words. He later introduced me to his global manager, and we are now looking at a very large nationwide opportunity—one that is worth a lot of money. And it all came from a simple APS delivered in the midst of a chaotic trade show.

In another situation, I had a slightly different experience. The vice president at a major security manufacturing company had asked me to speak at his national partner conference. The dates didn't work for me, so I had to decline. But as I was planning my 2007 speaking calendar, I called him. His administrative assistant informed me my contact was no longer there, but a replacement had started two weeks ago. She patched me through, and I found myself talking to the new VP of marketing.

At some point in the conversation, I mentioned the word "training" (immediate delegation to the training department). I felt myself sinking, but quickly reacted with the APS, "You know how…" I mentioned some of the issues her channel was facing. Her excitement seemed to kick in as she said, "Yes, that is the issue."

"That is what I focus on," I replied.

She immediately changed her tone and invited me to take a look at some slides she was preparing for the upcoming XChange conference in Chicago. She was asking me to become an advisor.

There were several points I didn't agree with, having worked with many resellers around the country. When we were done, she said, "I want to meet with you when I return." She was inviting me to continue in that advisory role, and I was asked to share my value proposition.

This brings us to the next step: We must have an answer. If people are going to ask us for the value prop, it must be good.

Building an Effective Value Proposition

Once your APS is perfected, people will ask you for your value proposition. In fact, it is important that you constantly test the APS questions you come up with to see how people respond. Are they asking for more, or are they exchanging a pleasant smile and walking away? If they aren't asking, your questions need work.

But once they start asking, you will need a response. When the software channel executive asked, I only had one chance—and it had to be perfect.

The security value proposition is likely the most powerful value proposition available in today's market. But before we can actually build one, we need to review some of the theory behind it. First, let's look at how security is positioned in the market and how it can be changed to create more impact at the business level.

Don't Treat Security as an Insurance Sale

Many people have said security has no ROI. Others have come along and tried to show it does, or that there is a *return on not investing*. Both may hold some truth, but it's helpful to look at security in another way.

Consider a sport like rock-climbing. If you climb, you know it involves equipment, your body and the rock. The climber wants to do something that, in many ways, seems to be impossible. He takes on cliffs that are thousands of feet tall and overhangs that defy gravity. He may spend his nights sleeping while suspended from ropes anchored by small metal objects placed in rock cracks.

To achieve this, the climber invests in ropes, camming devices (chocks in the old days), carabiners that clip things together, special shoes, a helmet and a sling.

When the ascent begins, the climber wears the harness and begins to place metal anchors into the rock as he works his way up.

With the exception of the shoes, the gear is never actually used to support the climber, unless he falls. All gear is designed for safety—not insurance.

If the climber falls, the rope, belayed by a teammate, will tighten, held by the anchors in the rock, and will support the climber, stopping the fall. He invests in safety so he can mitigate risk and decrease danger.

This analogy carries over to corporations looking to extend their safe business practices into less secure environments that will produce greater profitability—for instance, sending a sales force on the road to access secure corporate systems from insecure wireless locations like airports, coffee shops, hotels and even citywide wireless access points. Businesses may allow guest users, third-party processing companies, supply chain management applications and customer online access. All of these activities expose the company to the risk of unauthorized users gaining access through compromised systems.

Rock climbers want to purchase safety equipment. They look for new technologies that will provide greater security, allowing them to take on bigger challenges. The change from chocks to cams in the mid-'80s, for example, was an expensive upgrade for most of us, but we went for it, knowing these new devices would be less likely to fail. We could then take greater chances out on the rock face.

If we can convince our customers to view security in this way, there's an opportunity to apply the security/safety net to new business applications, enabling them to reach farther than they ever imagined.

Take a moment and consider several accounts you are working with right now. Every business that uses technology in any significant way is doing things to extend its business—to reach out to new markets, collaborate with partners who many times also compete, or perhaps outsourcing or offshoring to gain efficiencies in manufacturing or call center activities. All of these things introduce new levels of risk.

What are your clients doing with their business to become more competitive or more efficient, which at the same time introduces risk?

Write down several ideas. We will use them to create an effective, business-focused value proposition.

What Is Unique About Your Organization?

The next step, before we can actually build the value proposition or an opening to a more formal dialogue about your value, must be to understand what's really unique about your company. Have you ever tried to make a list of things that are truly unique about your organization? It's not an easy task. When I work with manufacturers, I hear comments like, "We have an end-to-end solution" or "Our support is better than any other company's." Perhaps they say, "Our thought leadership is better" or "We are setting the standards in the industry." When I hear this, my immediate thought is: "How will the executive of a large corporation receive these ideas?"

Do you have security solutions that span the network, mainframe, operating systems, applications, databases and end users? When you really think about it, there aren't too many true end-to-end solutions out there. Or, how about "best customer support, leadership and expertise?" Can you really make this claim—and can you prove it? You probably can't.

How about resellers? Do you have the best people, support or another unique qualification? In most cases, these things don't work.

As a manufacturer, you have to consider the security aspects you can provide that no other company offers—perhaps a set of products that work together in a unique way. If you work for an operating-system company like Microsoft or provide one of the various UNIX platforms, you can claim you're the only one who can really secure that system. Or, if you are a storage or network manufacturer, you may be able to claim that only you can provide security inside the devices you sell, thus leveraging the infrastructure in which the client has already invested.

As a reseller, you may have a particular methodology that has been developed to assess security. You may have a specialized security managed-services program developed for a certain market—perhaps even a vertical market. These are all unique.

In either type of company you have references. Everyone has references, but your references are unique. Your team's experience is unique to your company. And while other companies may make similar claims, the culture you build—whether an advantage or a liability—is, in fact, unique. Get a list. Brainstorm and come up with ideas that make you unique, and start building more differentiation into your company.

But at the top of the list is *you*—you as a trusted advisor. If you take the time to become the advisor—if you start identifying and memorizing the sound bites—you will be unique. Most salespeople won't do this, so take a step past your competitors and equip yourself with the one thing executives will notice.

What Interests Executives?

Now, with some level of differentiation, you need to ask the question: "What's really interesting to executives?" Again, a list is important. You have only one chance to connect with these people, and it has to be perfect. Over the last two years, I have compiled a list from technology sellers all over the country. Here's a partial list of what we came up with:

- Security trends—what's really happening globally
- What peers and competitors are doing to reduce risk
- How companies are reducing the cost of security
- Where and why security strategies are failing
- How to reduce the risk of exposure
- How to reduce the liability associated with loss
- The futures—where security and cyber-crime are headed
- What is hype, and what is reality?

These areas continue to be interesting to executives. As I get involved in marketing events, seminars and other speaking opportunities, I consistently find executives are willing to attend events where we address these issues. On the other hand, when I speak at or attend events that are more application-oriented or product-focused, the audience is almost completely made up of technical non-decision makers.

With this in mind, look back at your recent meetings. Are these the topics you're leading with, or are you resorting to PowerPoint slides, product data sheets and other technical information?

In my experience, most salespeople focus on the wrong issues, leading with their comfort zone and pushing the products with which they have been working. These conversations quickly move to the technical audience, leaving the decision makers out of the heart of the meeting. It's an immediate delegation back to the IT group.

In the next chapter, we will take a look at when and how to get their technical people involved, but at this stage our focus is on creating a vision for security at a business level—a vision in the mind of the asset owner.

The Components of Your Value Proposition

We can now begin to build our value proposition. The APS may have been used in a brief introduction, or someone may have sponsored you to meet with senior managers, economic buyers or high-level influencers. However you got the meeting, you now have one chance to make it count. So, what do you do?

Let's face it, every sales methodology out there calls for meeting the decision maker or economic buyer. While I agree with this process, it means you and every other salesperson in the market-place are calling one of two key individuals on every deal. The result? Thousands of salespeople are calling on a few key executives, who are tired of meeting salespeople with nothing important to say. The bottom line: You really need something great.

I've developed a short, five-point outline for the value proposition that takes the focus off the product (and the product people in the room), while placing the emphasis on key business systems and data. This immediately calls for the executive's attention.

Let's look at the outline:

- Security Trends
- What I See (Impact)
- My Concern
- What We Are Doing
- Specific to You

Security Trends. Security trends are a great place to start. We covered much of this in earlier chapters, but current news is important. This is not a scare tactic, but an articulation of the power, resources and determination behind organized crime, identity theft and the lucrative business of cyber-criminals.

People love news. We have 24/7 news channels, all kinds of newspapers and magazines and hours of talk radio, all delivering updates and commentary. Current security news gives your audience something relevant and interesting to focus on, while linking it to the systems and risk your prospect may be up against.

What I See (Impact). Working each day in the systems and network environment, you should be seeing the impact of these trends. Your consultants are likely watching as companies are hit with data loss, system outage, liability exposure, failed audits and possible business failure when they don't take the necessary steps to secure their systems and data. Review this with your prospect in a few short sentences to show you're witnessing the "bad guys" winning this battle.

My Concern. Security is your global humanitarian concern. At this point, you might want to shed a tear (not literally, but verbally). You should be passionate about people taking action, showing the same zeal as those who want to save trees, animals, starving children and cancer patients.

You need to convey the following message: If someone doesn't come up with a way to stop security breaches, U.S. companies could go out of business, banks could fail, and utilities could face major outages. Your personal identity could be stolen, and people could destroy your credit ratings, costing you lots of recovery time and money. Remember, more than 100 million identities in the United States have been exposed in the last two to three years. That's about one-third of our total population! This is a serious issue.

What We Are Doing About It. Someone has to solve your clients' problems. The steps companies are currently taking are failing. Data is being compromised, identities are being stolen, and information is being misused. Your company must build or supply some unique solution.

Remember the house model: protection, detection, response. These are the key aspects of security. How is your company working toward fixing the problem? Are you building security right into your product or providing a way for smaller organizations to affordably apply the right kind of security? This is where you articulate that value differentiation list we made a few pages back.

Specific to You. The last part of this meeting involves applying your solution in a way that motivates the client to spend the next 30 minutes talking about his problems and your solutions. Look back at the safety issues you came up with for your client. Are they worth spending 30 minutes on? If they are business-oriented, relevant issues, your prospect should have no problem spending at least 30 minutes looking at how your offerings fit with his business direction.

Build it—Memorize It!

Now that you have an outline, here comes the hard part: writing a compelling value proposition.

An example for a typical network company or solution

provider might look something like this:

Before we talk about our company and what we offer, I'd like to take a minute to share with you what we're seeing. Security challenges are changing. Identity theft is growing at an alarming rate, as organized crime recognizes it as a multibillion-dollar market. As with drug trafficking years ago, they are building huge programmer work forces to take control of companies like yours.

While we are not seeing as many viruses and worms disrupting our clients' networks and systems, we are seeing cyber-criminals break in using more effective stealth approaches to take control of systems and capture data, money and information. We are seeing large companies compromised, with no time to react! The criminals are winning this war right now.

I am concerned as I observe our national accounts experiencing these types of problems. Last year, more than 300 companies reported identify-theft incidents, but what about all of the companies that don't even know they have been compromised? It is estimated that 6 percent of all corporate computers, and perhaps 60% of the computers outside corporate walls, are controlled by software agents as part of a botnet.

At our company we are very concerned about this. We have dedicated vast resources and money to fix this issue. We believe that if we can build the security to stop such threats into the infrastructure or network you have already purchased, many of these problems can be eradicated. If we create a way to detect and respond to infected computers, unauthorized users and others with malicious intent, before they reach your data, we can stop much of what we're seeing.

As I've worked with your company, I see you use a lot of third-party processing. You use business process outsourcing and supply chain applications. Some of the advances we are making in this area of security can greatly enhance the level of security in your organization. In the same way you are protecting systems and servers with antivirus and spyware protection, we can protect the actual network within your organization. I would like to spend the next 30 minutes to examine how this may apply to your business more specifically and, if it makes sense, create some next steps. How does this sound to you?

It Must Be Predictable

Be willing to spend sufficient time on your proposition. It must read well to get the response you're looking for, and you have to deliver it as though it's a part of you. As with any successful movie, the script has to be developed, and the actor needs to study and memorize it. Finally, it has to be rehearsed. Then, as you deliver it, it will adapt. You will ultimately be capable of changing it as new situations arise. Above all, don't be lazy here. Many people assume they can pull it off without preparing. They think they can wing it. But can you imagine watching a movie with no script, where the actors make up dialogue as they go along? I'm guessing it wouldn't be a hit.

Your proposition must sound as though it came from you—not from your marketing group.

Set Up the Meeting to Ask Questions

Your value proposition sets the agenda, naturally leading to the first question: "What are you trying to protect?" It moves you from product to asset, starting with the news and ending with a business application. The first question then reinforces this move, shifting conversation away from the technical people in the room and toward the businesspeople who can make buying decisions.

You can then ask the second question: "What are the relevant threats?" This prompts data owners to share the areas in which they feel vulnerable.

Finally, you will ask: "How comfortable are you with your organization's ability to detect and respond to attacks?"

These questions uncover the critical assets, relevant threats and the company's posture, which helps you build the Impact Versus Likelihood Graph (right).

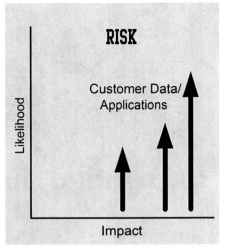

This is a dialogue—a rapport-building process that allows you to exchange ideas and see the situation from the client's perspective. Once you have this, it's time to start bringing things to a close with some action items. "Discussion" comes from a word that means "to end the dialogue"—and it's time for discussion and the house model.

The House, The Cloud and The Coverage Model can now be used to show clients where their security strategies are weak, how easy it is to break in and what holistic security should look like. From here, we will look at what to do with this information and how to create justification to move security initiatives forward.

Summary

- ☑ Use your positioning statement to create better introductions.
- ☑ Develop a list that differentiates your company and offerings. Focus on these items.
- ☑ Create a second list of things that interest executives and decision makers. Spend your meeting time on these topics, rather than your products.
- ☑ Build an effective value proposition using the outline provided.
- ☑ Improve, memorize and adapt your value proposition to meet the needs of your meetings.
- ☑ Use your value proposition to earn the right to ask questions.

Chapter 7

Creating Justification

How do I justify unbudgeted security projects?

When you have successfully moved your client away from thinking "product" and toward the risks associated with assets, you must provide a clear business justification for pursuing security solutions.

When you have successfully moved your client away from thinking "product" and toward the risks associated with assets, you must provide a clear business justification for pursuing security solutions.

Once you begin meeting with people, expect to be invited back on a regular basis.

So, where do you take these meetings? If compliance and cyber-crime are not sufficient motivators, what will create the justification for a security sale?

There are two scenarios:

1. A demand generation effort through which you educate business leaders and existing customers, either through events or personal visits

2. A client initiative that calls for new applications, expansions

in computing capabilities, or mergers and acquisitions

In either case, asset risk levels are affected, and there's an opportunity to review key concepts with clients. Notice that we're not waiting for them to initiate the requisition of security product. That's the third way to sell, but not a good one. It becomes a price war.

When to Bring the Proposal

Most sales start with the influencer. All salespeople say they call on C-level people; it's on their resumes. But realistically, the IT manager or IT personnel are the folks who are willing to take the meetings, and you have to start somewhere. This is not necessarily bad, but it needs to be approached correctly. For instance, if a lead comes in from a partner, general event or trade show, a custodian is the person who will look at available technology, seek education and request free evaluation equipment. But security, as I've previously indicated, is not sold to IT or security people, but to the person with liability.

If there's interest at the end of the influencer meeting, your client/prospect may ask for information. This is an interesting moment in the meeting, as non-decision makers are just that: They can't make a decision. So, they're sitting with you, interested in your offerings, and they know you want to do something that eventually turns into a sale. They don't want to admit that they are, in fact, powerless.

As the salesperson, you're looking for direction. You need to know if a lead is worth pursuing, and you want your prospect to provide some indication of the next step. What do you do?

The answer should be obvious: You need to find the asset owner. The person you are talking to can likely help you get there, but convincing him to do this requires some finesse. You can't force this individual to admit he has no power. I like to think of the sales process in four key meetings—four steps I need to complete the sales process. I recommend going into this process with these four meetings in mind, with the goal of getting a signature in four client meetings.

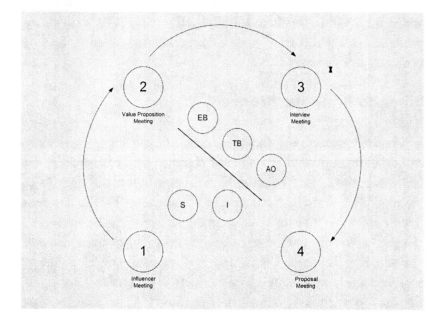

Meeting One: The Influencer Meeting

This is the first meeting in the sequence. It comes from other work your company has with this account, a marketing event where someone technical has shown up or a person you spoke with when cold-calling. We can hope this technical person is not a dedicated security resource. Remember, contrary to normal procedure, you don't sell security to the security people.

The goal of this meeting is simple: to arrange the second meeting with the asset owner or decision maker. Actually, there are four people you should identify, who are pictured in the diagram above. Most sales cycles begin and end with this influencer: the Sales person (S) meeting with the Influencer (I). The end comes when the influencer asks for pricing or more information; the sales process never really goes anywhere from here, simply because the person you are dealing with has no decision-making power. In my experience, about 10 percent of these deals actually close.

The four key people are: the economic buyer (EB), asset owner (AO), technical buyer (TB) and your coach (usually the initial meeting contact). There may be some overlap, but at the end of the first meeting, you need to know who all four people are. I define them as follows:

Economic buyer: The person who can say yes when everyone else says no. Depending on how expensive your offering is, this person may be lower or higher in the organization.

Asset owner: Up until now, we have treated him almost as the decision maker, and many times a decision maker will be a kind of asset owner. But the asset owner is really a person with liability. There may be more than one, but the key is to find someone who will drive the vision from a business level—someone who will be liable if things don't go right.

> **The goal of meeting 1 is to set up meeting 2 with the decision maker and asset owner.**

Technical buyer: This person is a key player in influencing the decision. Every economic buyer has a person he trusts—a person he will consult before making a big purchasing decision. While we don't want to propose pricing to this person, we will need him later in the sales cycle—specifically, in the third meeting.

Coach: This may be the influencer, but it may not. Early in the sales process, you need someone who will provide insider information. This should not be a new concept to any salesperson.

If this cannot be done, find out who you can meet with—preferably someone who can help you secure an appointment with the asset owner. Expect this to happen 50 percent of the time.

If the meeting goes well, your contact will ask for information or a proposal. Simply say: "Absolutely. Here is what I need to get this to you." Practice this line, as you will need to use it frequently. The goal, of course, is to have steps in mind to help you meet the right person. If you hand over the proposal at this point in the process, you lose control of the sales cycle.

Meeting Two: The Value Proposition Meeting

The next step is the value proposition meeting, where you meet with key influencers and the asset owner/decision maker. You will use your polished value proposition to demonstrate your understanding of the client's business, while identifying or clarifying the real assets for the buyer. From there, you exchange ideas on the relevant risks.

The key to this meeting is to focus on the asset owner and decision maker. This is not a technical meeting, and while there will likely be technical people in the meeting, your goal is for them to be bored—to drift off and not participate. Focus on the assets, not the products.

The goal of this meeting is to create a vision of your solution in the client's mind. You may be selling various types of technology, but the vision is focused on asset protection within the context of your other solutions.

Once the decision maker likes what you're saying, you have initially sold him, but he will want pricing. My response: "Absolutely. Here is what I need…"

Having identified the key influencers and potential asset owners, I tell them I need to speak to them individually by phone. If they don't agree to a short phone call, I know they're not serious.

If they're serious, they will spend another 10 minutes with me by phone. My justification is simple: I want to be sitting in front of my computer with my proposal questions so I have the details accurately reflected in my deliverables.

What I am really doing is separating people from the group so I can better discern where they stand. These phone meetings become my third meeting.

Meeting Three: The Interview

I start by calling the buyer: the decision maker. We refine the final scope, talk value, discuss budget and I attempt to upsell. Once we agree, I know I can get the others' buy-in. I've already set a date with the buyer, so I invite the others to join us in that meeting. I don't really care if they can make it, but the invitation has been extended.

When the calls are completed and I have everyone onboard, I can write the proposal with confidence. Writing before this step has been accomplished would be a waste of time.

Meeting Four: The Formal Proposal

The final step is simple. Everyone has verbally agreed to the project. If people haven't agreed, I remain at Step 3 until they do. There is no reason to write a proposal so people can just think about it. Sometimes a white paper, or what one colleague calls an idea paper, is a valid step, but it wouldn't contain prices, parts and everything you need to shop it.

This meeting is a delivery of the paper and a chance to remind everyone of the value proposition. I spend very little time on price and more time on what was said in past meetings. This meeting is designed to make people comfortable with their purchase. With your proposal in hand, review the justification, asset risks and price, and then return to value.

Using Assessments to Justify Spending

I recommend that your first sale with this client be an assessment. For decades, salespeople have used assessments to justify spending, so this is not a new concept. But not every assessment will lead to financial justification. By doing this, you avoid the long sales cycles associated with large product sales or even new technology or project sales. The sales time is spent selling a small assessment that's easy to approve without going to the board. Once in motion, justification can be established for an unlimited number on projects and services to follow. We will cover this in more detail in Chapter 8.

Let's take a look at how assessments are conducted and what constitutes a strong business case for moving security projects forward. While it is not within the scope of this book to explain the full assessment process and deliverables, it's important to differentiate it from routine vulnerability assessments frequently delivered to the IT organization.

When I was working with the small bank referenced in Chapter 5, the executive VP asked me for my recommendation on where his company should go after the first meeting, toward the end of my house analogy. How could he move from a protection-only strategy to the PDR model I described? I recommended an assessment; however, it occurred to me he might have already conducted one.

"If you already have this type of data, I can use it," I told him. "But first let me review some of the different approaches security providers take when performing an assessment to see if your data will meet our needs."

Vulnerability Assessment

I first addressed vulnerability. When consultants perform a security assessment, they usually focus most of their efforts on discovering vulnerabilities, which may include unpatched systems, misconfigured firewalls, sloppy application security or a lack of hardening on the servers, among other issues.

While the vulnerability assessment has some value, most lies in collecting information to be used in a more comprehensive analysis. For security, however, few consultants understand how to turn data into business-level justification. As a result, vulnerabilities are prioritized (maybe) and delivered in a technical document to the IT organization. These results frequently are relegated to someone's shelf.

A visit to one's physician provides a good analogy. Imagine going to the doctor and asking him to assess your body. You may ask him to run a bunch of tests and provide a list of every vitamin deficiency, germ to which you've been exposed, cancer risks, or problems that could occur if you fell, ate the wrong thing or were involved in an accident. This list would obviously be quite long, and almost useless. I suspect you, too, would shelve it and forget about it.

Penetration Test

Sometimes used interchangeably with vulnerability assessments, a penetration test, or pen test, is really quite different. Here, you're focusing on specific systems or data, with the intent to break in. A client may hire you to try to steal data (sometimes called trophies) to see if you can break through security barriers.

Pen tests are not inexpensive, and they require some advance planning to make sure business isn't disrupted. But in the drive to sell products, solutions and perhaps managed services, this test often is not a great method of providing justification. In fact, all it does is prove what we already know: that someone out there can break in. And if we can't get through, it merely means we didn't have the right people on our team. The client has gained nothing from this.

"I can do a pen test for free," I told the VP in our meeting. "Someone can get in. It may not be me, but there is someone who can do it. Given enough time, all systems can be broken."

This point isn't that we can keep everyone out. Rather, can we detect and respond before data is stolen or compromised?

Security Audit

Audits are the third type of assessment. They are particularly important because the process conflicts with most security purchases. Some clients ask me whether performing the assessment and selling a product are a conflict of interest. If any conflict exists, it's the audit, but the client doesn't always have a strong bias about it. He's asking me to justify my approach. And when this happens, I know I'll gain his business if I can prove my point.

Audits are performed by people hired to inspect networks and systems. They have required standards, used to see if their clients pass the test. If a client's system fails, the auditor provides a report on noncompliant areas.

I urge resellers to refrain from getting involved in audits. You want product business that has the potential to become monthly revenue and renewal business, which builds company valuation over time.

Risk Assessment

While many reports are called risk assessments, few offer any measurement of risk (the measure of impact versus the likelihood something bad will happen). Certainly, there are more complete definitions that take into consideration business impact (quantitative and qualitative measurements of downtime and disruption), annual rates of expectancy and other risk-related factors. But the goal here is not to build a practice around security assessments, but to build the program. The risk-assessment process creates the justification required to move the program forward.

Rather than delivering a heavyweight document and charging by the pound, I hope to deliver a fairly simple, yet relevant, document that helps data owners understand where they are at risk, which threats are relevant and where to apply their dollars toward the security relevant to their business requirements.

Here's a simple formula to follow:

1. Focus on assets. Remember Question 1: "What are you trying to protect?" This question was created to move the conversation away from products and toward assets. Now that we've identified the asset and successfully transitioned our attention from the data custodian to the data owner, it will be important to keep it there. The report must be written specifically with this person in mind. Supporting data can be delivered to the custodians.

2. Address the entire system. Traditional security assessments often focused on perimeter issues, inside or outside security controls, or perhaps the entire enterprise. This approach may work for certain applications, but not for what I propose here. By entire system, I mean the servers, networks and connectivity associated with a particular set of assets—something tightly defined that can be accomplished in a short amount of time, but will have great impact.

Trusted systems, all points of access, policies, procedures and anything that may affect assets on a given system are relevant. I'm not saying you must assess the entire organization; rather, take some of the key systems and address all relevant aspects.

3. Focus on business processes. The focus here is on asset loss or compromise. Business processes and critical systems, including security controls, change control, users and data sources, become relevant to assessing the likelihood of data loss, integrity loss or data availability.

4. Consider relevant threats. There are numerous issues with every system, so relevancy is important. When you have a health exam, you don't want a list of every potential issue or a test for every disease known to mankind. Rather, you want to know if you face any immediate dangers. Banks, pharmaceutical companies and manufacturers face different threats. This addresses the answer to question two in the four principles for communicating with asset owners: What are the relevant threats?

5. Prioritize according to business impact. Clients can help weight the importance of the systems involved, but it's up to the consultant to prioritize the issues based on impact and likelihood.

6. Deliver measurable risk. Showing the data owner the risks in graphic form provides value. Show your method, and justify your findings. Your deliverable here is simple: an executive looking at the risk graph (right).

7. Create a continuous process. This may be the most important point on this list. Selling a one-time assessment raises awareness, but quarterly updates allow you to manage the remediation process. Selling the client on doing the baseline and then adding a quarterly update (a brief walkthrough) allows you to review new projects, system changes, and future plans to identify issues and concerns. At the same time, as an advisor, you have the opportunity to remind clients of the potential dangers, helping them plan continuously and purchase the roadmap you're laying out. Without this last step, you will likely lose your momentum with this account.

Using the Risk Assessment

Risk assessments are performed by companies that specialize in information security, frequently sold as an unbiased look at how secure a given company's systems are. Many people have asked me how to overcome objections to a single company performing this assessment, only to be followed by proposals to sell products. Can one company do both?

The answer is an emphatic yes. Security boutique companies

will use this unbiased line to make the sale, and it is fair to do so. These companies depend on their security expertise and methodology to close business; it's part of their sales strategy. It's no different from the point product strategy used to bring security discussions and product evaluations down to a feature/function battle when pitching a one-product company with a unique high-tech solution (the counter being a high-level, business-oriented vision sold to executives).

Consider the alarm salesperson. He comes to your home; walks through your halls, garage and around the back of the house; and begins pointing out where the holes are. He shows you how easy it is to break in, basically performing a free assessment. If he is really good at what he does, he will convince you that your home is unsafe. He has essentially become your trusted advisor. The sale is made by showing you how the impact can be avoided by reducing the likelihood of an attack or intrusion.

At this point, the salesperson becomes your consultant and begins to design your security system. He takes the data from the free assessment, and he looks at the location of doors, windows and other points of entry. He reviews your home's construction, location, neighborhood, lighting and visibility to other homes, and he comes up with a design consisting of door sensors, window sensors, glass break sensors and motion detection. For higher-end implementations, he may toss in video surveillance and, in the end, may sell you a managed services program (24/7 monitoring, with no guarantees).

It would be rare to hire an outside firm with no security products to design this system. You look to the manufacturer or value-added reseller to understand the risks, what products offer and perform the installation.

An assessment is not an audit, in this case, but a process that takes the client from conception to implementation, and all the way to a managed service program. I cannot think of one assessment I've sold, with this concept in mind, that hasn't led to product sales.

Delivering Value to the Data Owner

The critical factor in everything I've discussed is the deliverable. Once you're established as the consultant who performs the assessment, the relationship must remain at the data-owner level. This means technical people perform the information-gathering at the technical levels, deliver technical assessment materials and are available to explain their findings.

Concurrently, you are working with your higher-level consultants at the business level to understand the applications, data value, impact of an issue and likelihood of things going bad. Your primary deliverable is written with the data owner and business executive in mind, using charts, pictures and bullet points to communicate clearly what the client must do to reduce exposure.

Formal presentations are used to explain what you found, recommend action steps based on impact numbers or weightings and justify your recommendations. A roadmap is used to paint a picture of what could be and how the enterprise may be extended to new markets where computing is unsafe, if necessary. This may include accessing intranet portals and email from the local coffee shop.

Subscription Programs

The subscription is the final factor in selling your program—a critical part of driving the roadmap. Most companies will not purchase large security remediation projects the day after you deliver your findings. Sales approached from the angle taken in this book target new opportunities and unbudgeted initiatives. The idea is to get the client to see something for which he isn't already creating RFPs.

The subscription gives you control over future project initiatives. Every month/quarter, you're back in front of the managers, reviewing new projects and system changes that affect the overall security architecture and represent new levels of risk. At the same time, you are reminding them of the exposure they already have given no remediation efforts.

This is not a time to sell hard, but to continually position your company as a trusted advisor. Done right, you should find yourself invited to planning sessions, company meetings, and opportunities to present your findings and recommendations to other executives (and, potentially, board members).

Each quarter, you should update what you have and expand your view into the client's computing environment. Every project, system change, or application addition or enhancement is potentially an increase in the existing project's scope. Updates represent reminders of the progress toward remediation, while scope expansions introduce you to new projects that may provide opportunities for other company offerings. Of course, scope changes should also represent fee changes.

The bottom line: Use the subscription process to expand your presence, deliver greater value and position your company as the go-to provider for maintaining data availability, confidentiality and integrity on any part of the client's infrastructure. This is not a pure security product sale; it touches every aspect of creating, using, transmitting, storing, archiving and disposing of mission-critical corporate data assets.

Summary

- ☑ Justification is required when creating new opportunities.
- ☑ All assessments are not equal. Focus on the risk assessment.
- ☑ Unbiased assessments are not necessary. Sell against them by educating the customer.
- ☑ Sell the program. Use a subscription service to expand your presence and scope within the account.
- ☑ Focus your deliverables on data owners, while positioning the technical resources of your organization with IT.

Chapter 8

The Winning Proposal

How do you turn the hearts of senior executives, high-powered influencers and economic buyers?

In *The Fifth Discipline,* author Peter Senge reveals that people will die for a well-formed vision. When they understand current realities, see the possibilities of what could be and believe in their advisors' ability to take them there, they'll make the journey.

I once saw persuasion defined as "guiding truth around others' mental roadblocks." Sales are made using the justification and guidance you provide through the assessment process described in the last chapter. Once you have justification, the sale can be made. It's the art of persuasion that allows you to show buyers the truth in ways that allow them to make buying decisions.

Everything starts with a new understanding of the risks involved in running a business dependent on mission-critical assets. The prospect agrees threats are changing; protection, detection and response are necessary to the security architecture; and his current strategy bought into the idea that protection alone would be sufficient to guard his most precious assets.

Perhaps he has hired you to assess risk; show him, based on provided impact data, the likelihood of a breach; and help him prioritize certain systems in terms of risk.

Reading the Risk Assessment

Over the last two years, I've asked many security professionals—from product manufacturers, software developers, solution providers, security boutiques, large integrators, and smaller midmarket and SMB solution providers/resellers—where they find their greatest opportunities. Where are the big holes in the average security architecture? Here's what they have said:

Policy. While most companies have a security policy, many do not update it on a regular basis. Employees may be required to read it, but tracking is inadequate, and the average policy lacks the supporting standards, guidelines and procedures. Across the board, policies lack enforcement, reducing them to a set of guidelines. They don't necessarily limit liability and drive architecture, as they're designed to do.

Segmentation. Internal networks are treated as one big trusted family. Regardless of division lines, data sensitivity in financial or manufacturing locations, and regulatory requirements like HIPAA or GLBA, companies have failed to provide segmentation among divisions requiring different degrees of security. Even with voice networks—a logical part of the design—companies have been remiss and/or noncompliant. One of the best examples is higher education: Administrative and financial systems are on the same network as faculty and student records—three groups, requiring three very different levels of security, all in one segment separated by passwords.

Applications. Web applications are particularly deficient when it comes to security. While there are application testing tools from companies like SpiDynamics, as well as application-specific fire-walls, many companies aren't using them, and they don't require security to be built into the application. I've had conversations with third-party application developers who say it's just too cost-ly and time-consuming to put security into the application. They recommend that clients ensure a safe environment by using fire-walls and other security devices. This is unbelievable and unac-ceptable.

IP-Telephony. This is another example of an application—one that may perhaps be the creator and transmitter of some of the most critical information in the organization. This is where com-panies handle mergers and acquisitions, stock trades, employee decisions, changes to key products, new ideas—in short, the future of the organization. Why do so many companies assume this is a safe place to create and transmit highly sensitive infor-mation?

System Security. Large servers are connected to web applica-tions, allowing third-party processing, customers, internal users, external users and anyone else to create or interact with data. Assessments have shown system security is generally weak, granting users complete access (including creation, read, write and deletion rights) to key data. Passwords may allow guest access; user IDs often remain active after employees are gone; and, as jobs change and needs evolve, users' access rights often become out of step with their needs. Some administrators create back doors or trusted relationships among systems to ease their burden, but wind up creating significant weaknesses in the secu-rity architecture.

Remote Access. Remote access always seems to be a problem. Workstations and PDAs access mission-critical data from just about anywhere, day and night. Systems used at home by children and spouses for chatting, blogging, shopping and other recreation are then used to access corporate systems. Laptops are accessing these same systems from airports, hotels, coffee shops and public hotspots without any concern for privacy. Simple passwords, POP3 protocols, webmail and instant-message applications are used to transmit highly sensitive information in the clear.

Portable Data Systems. Another laptop/PDA problem exists when we consider the safety of data as it leaves the enterprise. A recent *USA Today* article described how a company performed a study on data security and mobile devices. After purchasing 10 cell phones from eBay, the firm showed how carelessly people dispose of data. With some Internet and homegrown tools, they were able to recover enough information to print an eight-foot stack of 8.5" by 11" documents, with information that included Social Security numbers, account numbers, credit card information, sales efforts, and merger and acquisition information from text-message sessions. In most cases, the phones had been erased, yet the data was recoverable.

Wireless. Despite the endless stories about war driving, people still opt for the ease of unencrypted wireless access. Other wireless networks may have been encrypted using the WEP protocol, but never updated. Many voice applications now use wireless. With a simple tool downloaded from the Internet, these wireless networks are easily compromised. People use them without realizing how insecure they are.

Partners, Guests and Contactors. While many companies have managed to secure the perimeter, back-door connections are often created to allow partners to share applications. Routers connect seemingly secure networks to other companies that may have lower security standards. Guests are provided full access to the network, with only a password standing between them and sensitive data. Contactors often have access to systems they maintain, with full administrative rights and no accountability.

Real-Life Situations

My own findings support the problems I've just identified. I recently received payment from a major global company through the Internet. I was sitting in an airport, accessing an insecure email account. One of my messages contained a client's credit card, security code and expiration date.

Another time, I was assessing a telecommunication company's security. The IT group had actually created segments going around the firewall to allow one of its applications to work correctly. It was a temporary solution, but it had been in place for more than a month.

One of my clients calls on a major software manufacturer that processes accounting data for small companies throughout the United States. A recent firewall issue threatened to shut down his software application. During a particularly busy time of year, the firewall manufacturer actually recommended that he pull out the firewalls temporarily and use access control lists in his routers until the problem could be solved.

It's been more than a month since he implemented this temporary fix—and these accounts hold all kinds of information that could be used by cyber-thieves to create new identities or apply for loans, among other risks.

Another client was donating PCs to charity without deleting data. He was erasing the disks, but studies show it's relatively easy to recover data from an erased disk.

While working with a regional bank, I discovered its primary banking applications, running on an AS/400, provided complete access to third-party processing companies. They had rights to not only read information, but to change or delete it. This bank also transmits account information across the Internet as part of its loan approval process—clearly a violation of GLBA.

I could go on, but you get my point. Security is weak, and much of the problem can be fixed without getting into highly technical details.

The Product List

When an assessment comes in with issues I've just discussed, your first inclination may be to start listing products. Take a look at the list of products you sell. There are likely many, some of which overlap; some more expensive; and some more relevant than others. You shouldn't view it as a product list, but as a component list.

A friend purchases and restores historical homes. When I first entered the last home he purchased—a 100-year-old house in South Carolina—I was amazed at the amount of work he faced. One of the obvious issues was electrical systems. With holes in the walls and missing light fixtures, you could see the wiring wouldn't meet state codes. I imagined what would happen if someone were standing in a puddle of water and turned on a faulty appliance—a disaster waiting to happen.

If I were an electrician, my first thought would be to assess the situation—to walk through, crawl through and inspect every part of the system. Going back to my truck, I would have numerous components to choose from to create a safe living environment.

You should view your component list in the same way. Don't call them solutions, as they're not. Don't think of them as products to place at a company. Components must carry the right connotation, instilling the idea that various products/integration, policies and education are required to create a safe computing environment. In fact, all nine boxes of the coverage model presented in Chapter 5 should be considered as one seamless system or security architecture.

Remote-Access Example

We've all sold VPNs. Let's assume a prospect comes to you and asks you to sell one. What's your response to this request? Some readers may ask how many ports are needed, how many users will use the system and which applications the client is planning to support. These questions result in delegation to the security team—again, not the place we want to start.

Try another approach. Ask: "What are you trying to protect?" Looking at the VPN solution, we can assume there's a need to access certain key systems remotely, but it can actually be done without the aid of a VPN. The VPN was introduced to provide some level of security. What does the VPN actually provide? Your first thought may be secure remote access, but does it accomplish this? Your second answer may be encryption of data between the endpoint and perimeter. This answer is correct, but how secure is it?

The fact is, encrypting data may make systems less secure. Of course, I'm exaggerating a bit to make my point. But because data cannot be seen, whatever is happening on an end-node is passing through the perimeter—perhaps to a DMZ area on the network, but through the firewall, without the ability to see what's coming in.

The solution is to add something to this picture. After I ask, "What are you trying to protect?", I have the information I need to start designing a more secure way to access data remotely. I may add some way to authenticate users with strong or two-factor authentication. A token or one-time password could be used.

Secondly, I should add some way to ensure end users' workstations have the right patches, are running the latest software versions and meet workstation configuration standards. I can do this with some type of network access control server.

It would be helpful to have some level of intrusion-prevention software running at the perimeter where data is deciphered, ensuring malicious traffic doesn't enter the corporation's trusted network. And don't forget a way to monitor activity: when users come in, who they are, what they do and when they leave. Accountability is important here. Is there real time monitoring and alerting, as well as an audit trail with which no one can tamper?

At the end-node, the operating system must be protected from all forms of malware, spyware and misuse. Several applications may be required to do this, and the prospect may have much of this in place. It is the salesperson's job, regardless of whether he sells these products, to recommend using them.

Wireless Application

With the remote access example, you will recommend some way to keep the end-node safe from malware and remote-control attacks by using antivirus, anti-spyware and perhaps some form of intrusion-prevention software. Your corporate network assessed the end-node's condition before allowing a connection to be established, you then checked with an access control server to ensure the user was authorized to come in. You determined the restrictions that should be applied to each session. You ensured the user was, in fact, who he claimed to be by using strong authentication. Finally, you provided encryption and some means of centrally managing this activity.

Moving to a wireless application, what would have to change? If you guessed nothing, you're right. It's the same scenario. The end user must be clean, authenticated, authorized and permitted; once connected, he must be monitored.

In fact, regardless of where this connection occurs (internal or external, wireless, partner, consultant, guest or other), the same steps are required. Encryption may not be required in some instances, and a simple password may work for some internal users. But, in general, you should recommend these basic safety controls if the user is going to achieve secure remote access, or secure access of any kind.

Systems and Storage

You may have opportunities with servers, storage and end-user devices. Each concept should be applied to the OS, application and database. Again, it's the same scenario of ensuring a clean system, authentication, authorization and event correlation. Encryption is applied to transmission, storage and archival.

In each case, the three pillars of security are applied: confidentiality, integrity and availability of the system and its data. In the network case, single points of failure are eliminated. In the systems and storage area, the same is true, with the added function of ensuring proper backups and restore capability.

If you have sold in the systems arena for any length of time, you should recognize that tapes often fail, and system failures often take far longer than the average four-hour response time to be placed back in full service. This is why Symantec bought Veritas in 2005. In its quest to secure data, operating systems and applications, it needed the capability to back up data and create a highly available configuration.

Voice Applications

Several features make VoIP attractive, including the managed services aspect and overall security. Note that security applies across the sale, from the initial voice sale to the managed services offering.

As mentioned earlier, voice has significant relevance with security. When people pick up the phone, they are convinced their conversations are off the record. And while some people send sensitive content via email, we are starting to catch on as people use email as an audit trail.

It's not that traditional analog voice applications couldn't be taped or recorded; they could and sometimes are. But the tools available today for network-hacking allow intruders to easily record voice along with data. And because we know bots and other malicious software products are being used across all infrastructure to steal information, we can be sure people are tapping into VoIP.

Companies that could be securing their voice are not. People who sell voice are not educating consumers on its risks in an effort to keep the sale moving. But this is a disservice to the customer and a missed opportunity to set yourself apart. It's easy to record voice on a network—to sit between two executive callers with a PC and capture information discussed regarding future mergers, big sales opportunities, coming layoffs or the latest product roadmaps.

Some of the simplest steps aren't being taken. Newer switch and router technologies are designed for voice to improve quality and give administrators the necessary security to keep an eye on their networks. Using simple logging tools, as well as centralized correlation and alerting, can go a long way, with network time protocols to ensure that logging is time-stamped properly to allow for precise correlation.

Phone gateways that provide for encryption should be used where communications are sensitive. This is certainly the case in any large or mid-size organization at the executive level. Encryption can be applied to certain parts of the network—for instance, between the CEO's and CFO's offices. In addition, certificates or software token passwords can provide secure login at phone stations. Phones are computers in this scenario, so it's important to guard against recording and people using this connection point to gain access to secure network resources.

IPS is an important tool, as well. While some calling applications come with scaled-down IPS software, mid-sized and enterprise-level businesses require greater protection. Without a full-blown IPS software solution, complete correlation of events is impossible. This is the key to applying the detection-response component of security architecture. Remember: Relying on protection is not good enough.

Further, it's becoming popular to build many of the security software features we see on PCs right into the network. Cisco and Juniper are heavily investing in building antivirus, anti-spyware, IPS, encryption, authentication and many other security controls into their products. They should be implemented when installing voice in any major corporation. It's even possible to add an inline sniffer into this type of configuration to ensure perpetrators aren't sneaking into secure parts of the voice or data network.

Finally, it has always been a best practice to lock down operating systems on servers, making sure guest access, general administrator access and OS services are kept to a minimum. This same consideration must be extended to phone systems. As these small computers that resemble phones are installed, they come with installation tools, web access and troubleshooting features that are often turned on. These systems must be locked down to ensure security. Access is possible from remote locations, exposing sensitive information to a variety of network resources.

Security can be achieved, but it takes thought and due care. Use phones that support higher levels of encryption, over and above WEP (the commonly used protocol that's easily cracked with downloaded tools). Use access points that utilize technologies that ensure rogue access points are not added to the wireless voice network. Employees sometimes add to the network simply to make their jobs easier; what they fail to understand is how they're exposing their companies to serious threats and liability.

I recently asked a security engineer who specializes in voice about the top four voice insecurities. Here's the list:

1. Insecure wireless/voice installations
2. Poor use of VLANs and router configurations with voice
3. Lack of locked-down systems
4. Relying on lower-end security features rather than adding more full-featured event detection tools

Three out of four are simple configuration issues. Only the last one requires additional products. But people don't think through the design and end up installing voice insecurely. It's only a matter of time before someone is listening in—and perhaps years before you find out.

Remember: Cyber-criminals are not looking to disrupt a business; they surreptitiously seek profits.

Selling the Solution

Given the assessment results, vendor-developed security strategies and your need to close the long-term security opportunity, your goal is to take your vision to the asset owner. Remember: Taking your recommendations to the security team, at this point, is a waste of time. They can't spend money, have their own biases and will ask time-wasting questions that confuse the sales process.

If you've completed the assessment process, you should have a strong rapport with the asset owner and other key influencers. Your technical people should have interacted with the client's technical people, and by default his security people. Maintain your executive peer relationship to clarify the buyer's vision of what could be.

In a recent follow-up program, I was asked why attendees consistently hit roadblocks, even when using these principles. I asked for a show of hands on how many people had developed a quality APS. Sadly, no one had.

I then asked how many had written, refined and memorized their value proposition. Several said they wished they had. Finally, I asked them to identify the asset owner. In most cases, they were still dealing with data custodians. That explains why salespeople were unsuccessful and why a follow-up program is needed.

You need accountability when implementing these steps, so form an accountability relationship with someone you trust as you execute these concepts. A sales coach is the best choice—someone who will hold your feet to the fire without worrying about offending you.

Presenting to Executives

Always start with the assets. Highly sensitive information and a company's understanding of exposure will sell solutions. Open with a restatement of your value proposition to remind clients of the trends, your concerns and your differentiation. Tie these to their initiatives and requirements to extend the enterprise.

Rather than referring to the network or CAD/CAM system, speak in terms of intellectual capital, customer data, strategic documents and liability. Stay away from technical topics, which will be addressed in a separate meeting with your technical experts. Focus on the answers given in Question 1: What are you trying to protect?

Relevant Threats

Extending the enterprise brings new risks and exposure. A review of these areas, supported by your assessment, will help clients see where they're exposed and where changes are needed. Validate your findings and the company's priorities to reach agreement and a common vision. Business threats include loss of customer confidence, market share, branding and reputation, and competitive advantage—not to mention the liability that comes with losing sensitive data.

Using the house or cloud illustrations, managers can visualize where sensitive data resides and how current computing practices and new company initiatives create greater exposure. This raises awareness of how vulnerable data is.

Creating the Vision

Begin your remediation plan with the area in which you have the least competition. Bringing up commodity products like antivirus, workstation intrusion protection, firewall and other tools available at Staples or CompUSA isn't a good place to start.

Highlighting security that can be added to infrastructure products you've previously delivered and implemented is a great place to start. If you've sold this client a network, perhaps it's time to upgrade security controls that can be built in or added to routers and switches.

Several years ago, when Cisco acquired Okena (its intrusion prevention agent, now called Cisco Security Agent or CSA), resellers were told to lead with this new silver bullet, claiming *Zero Day Protection.* This did not sell! Why? Intrusion prevention software is rapidly becoming a commodity that buyers expect to purchase as part of a suite of security tools. The moment someone brings up an IPS Software agent, the buyer thinks of workstation antivirus software ("Don't we already have that in our antivirus software?"). Recovering is almost impossible once you have challenged another decision made by the people in the room.

Changing your approach by focusing on router and switch security allows this same sale to head down a new path: "What if we could increase security by building it right into the fabric of your network, leveraging your existing investment, easing management and providing the capability to check users before they connect? We can ensure they are who they say they are, establish a secure encrypted session and monitor everything that happens during this connection.

If something malicious is detected, the network will have the intelligence to stop it, quarantine the user or, if required, upgrade or patch the system in question." This approach starts at the network's core, and it will elicit a much different response from the buyer.

The same can be done with storage systems. Rather than looking at the end-node for client protection, start with availability and integrity of data, encryption or backup-and-restore point objectives.

Companies like EMC have been doing this for years, avoiding price wars by selling availability and information management instead of disk space.

Servers can also be sold with security by focusing on availability and business continuity. Again, start where there is no competition, leveraging assets, data location and the need to build security into the infrastructure.

If you use the cloud diagram, decision makers can connect the last meeting, where they agreed to do the assessment, to the current meeting, where you are putting together the pieces that create a secure computing environment.

Product Overview

Avoid using acronyms and esoteric technological concepts. This is not executive vernacular, so they won't understand what you're telling them. Instead, relate your diagram to product concepts.

Remember: Certain words bring immediate delegation back to IT—a demotion for you. Other words wake up nearby technical people, while losing executives whose eyes glaze over. Don't fall into this trap.

For instance, software added to a client's network can process data, looking for malicious traffic and viruses. Firewall functions (a well-understood product) can be added to create segmentation within the network.

A small appliance may be added internally to create visibility into the client's systems, showing who's accessing what, when they're doing it and what they're actually doing while connected. This greatly reduces the risks associated with remote access, wireless computing and perhaps web-server interfaces. It's like setting up parent controls in your home so you know what your kids are up to on the Internet. In this case, we are managing identities.

By adding software to the remote client, we can create a shell around the operating system that doesn't allow anything to execute or operate that machine without the system administrator knowing about it and the user identifying himself.

Recommended Next Steps

The next steps are critical. If you don't recommend a path,

either the client will recommend one for you or there won't be one. The best path is receiving endorsement from the team that allows your technical experts to work with the client's technical team.

Your technical people should be equipped to bring insights to the IT organization. The company's team may be slow to give up its technology if it competes with yours, especially when brand loyalty has been established through gifts, golf and free lunches. Gain the sponsorship; then bring in the team.

Evaluations may be required. If so, develop a project plan to manage the process.

Don't install free products that people can play with at your expense, even if it's just an opportunity cost. Proof of concept, with preset milestones and agreed-upon next steps following the successful completion of predetermined objectives, should be your goal.

A Word on Discounts

This is not the time to discuss discounting products. Michael Bosworth offers a great analogy in *Solution Selling*, in which he compares discounting to a wet washcloth: Buyers will continue to squeeze as long as water comes out. Secure agreement on what the buyer really wants. Don't budge on price, or your product is purely a commodity.

Finally when everything is agreed to—when the vision is established—put it in writing. Take everything you have agreed to and document it. The sale is made in the presentation, not the paper document.

Keep documents short and to the point, assume the sale is made in the document, and have a place to sign off. For instance, write it as though it's signed: "We will be implementing the new security systems on the voice network using _____." Make it easy to buy, offer several options, and reiterate value until a contract is signed.

Summary

☑ Use assessment results to stay focused on assets.

☑ Consider the holistic security solution-all aspects of protection, detection and response in the scenario or application with which you are working.

☑ Construct a business-centric plan, leaving behind the technical jargon your competitors like to use.

☑ Develop a vision that enables the company to go beyond what a normal business can do by building in safety concepts.

☑ Present to the data owners—the people with liability.

☑ Trade short-term margin for long-term reoccurring revenue.

Chapter 9

Principles of Winning

**How do I win more security business
in a crowded market of
highly skilled competitors?**

Winning means moving away from product, finding
the assets and asset owner, and creating a vision
for security within the context of your client's
business model.

Most of the time, when we think about competition, we respond with the features and benefits that differentiate our company or product. If we're selling a product, we call in the engineers to argue functionality. If it's a service opportunity, we bring out our certifications, resumes, case studies and perhaps pricing. We sometimes have to respond to an RFP; other times, it's several companies bidding with their own proposals. Often, it comes down to commodity products at the lowest price.

In most of these cases, we're dealing with people who are acting on a preconceived notion of what they expect to see, and we're talking primarily to an influencer. There are millions of great reasons not to talk to the decision maker; if the average salesperson can come up with one, he will talk himself into using it. In some cases, this is OK, but it rarely results in a win in the security world.

If you're in the middle of a deal and turned to this chapter first, welcome to the book. There are a number of factors to keep in mind when working to win a client's business, but they're all based on chapters other readers have digested to get here. My advice? Start at the beginning.

I do not intend, in this chapter, to compare all of the technologies out there or turn this book into a Sales 101 class. I want to examine some of the strategies used by product manufacturers, look at the strengths and weaknesses of various business models, and bring you back to the foundational principles of justifying security and buying decisions.

Consider Deals You've Won

It's always a good idea to review the deals you've won. If you've had the opportunity to win a company over to your way of thinking in the security world, it's helpful to analyze how it happened. We're not talking about making a firewall sale, but convincing a buyer to invest in a more thorough security strategy or to consider security in buying decisions related to infrastructure sales. Perhaps you've sold an in-depth assessment that led to multiple remediation projects. More frequently, I meet people who have sold the assessment, but remediation projects did not follow. It is helpful to understand why.

Over the last year, I've talked with more than 400 salespeople about significant deals they've won. Many were unable to come up with one that represented a total mindset change on the customer's part. Those who could summon an example conveyed a consistent theme: They had a security vision for securing assets—one that involved moving from rank-and-file IT administrators to asset owners. Many leveraged their senior managers or business-savvy security consultants to form a vision for business success. In every case, the process moved the client away from technology and created a safe place to look at applications, assets and liability.

Case Study

I've sometimes started with a technical person who is considering a firewall upgrade or relicensing. A few years ago, I was brought in as the senior manager on an initially small firewall sales opportunity.

I agreed to attend the meeting on one condition: The buyer must be there. As the meeting opened, I did what I've done many times: I leaned over to my colleague and asked him to put the quote away. This was not a meeting for quotations. I knew that as soon as we pulled out a product quote, the meeting would transition from the buyer to the price and, finally, to the technology, where we'd be stuck for the remainder of the meeting. Once this happens, the decision makers check out, and the big opportunity is lost.

Addressing the economic buyer, I asked the first question: "What are you trying to protect?" As predicted and noted in previous chapters, the dialogue began. The data owner began to talk about applications and data. Sure, the technology people in the room tried to provide some answers, but I kept my focus on applications and data assets, refusing to get into a technical discussion. Facing the data owner, it was difficult for the IT representatives to take charge of the meeting. They tried, but didn't succeed.

After learning about the business, its critical systems and the importance of certain data maintained, I had a clear understanding of what was really important about this project. I knew the systems; understood the importance of the company's brand and its dependence on trust; and had a feel for how sensitive the data, its confidentiality, integrity and availability were. From there, we talked about relevant threats and the data owner's comfort level. I learned access control and availability were the primary considerations—not uncommon with many calls I've made. I now had a picture that described the data owner's impact versus likelihood graph—the company's risk model.

Still looking at the data owner, I commented on the firewall's role in providing the kind of security necessary to maintain a safe computing environment. It turned out, as it does in many cases, that the firewall was not the major requirement, but merely a supporting element of security at the perimeter. We spent the rest of the meeting talking about business continuity, access control, identity management and user awareness. The firewall people were bored, but content. I think they may have slept through the remainder of the meeting.

At the end of the meeting, the data owner was convinced we needed to look at these other areas and that some sort of short, high-impact assessment would help us pinpoint where to invest in security. In our recommendations, I verbally pointed out in a private phone call that the firewall he currently had in place was fine, but expensive and not highly available. The final deal included our recommendation on firewall technology, along with identity management, application security, remote connectivity security and managed services. We ate well at the end of the month.

The lesson here is simple: Ask the question, "What are you trying to protect?" Move the meeting from product to assets, and get the data owner to talk about what he needs to move his business forward.

Competing Product Strategies

If you're a reseller, you likely sell a number of products that overlap. If you work for a larger manufacturer, you may sell various security products or others that incorporate security. A smaller boutique security company may be focused on security aspects or a point product or technology. Each has a distinct strategy and will work to gain buy-in at different organizational levels. It's helpful to consider a variety of strategies to best position your offerings as you identify assets and build justification for investing in security.

The main issue is to avoid competing. As a solution provider, you want to stay away from commodity selling and price wars.

Vendor Business Models

As I flip through a copy of *SC Magazine,* I see ads from hundreds of security product companies, which can be broken down into three basic types:

Small, niche security product companies, with only one or two products to sell. These companies are often started by entrepreneurs with a technical bent. These individuals once worked for larger companies, had a great idea, and realized their only way to make money was to get out and start a new company. Their goal and strategy are important: At some point, they hope to sell the company to a larger one, similar to the one they left.

Larger security-only companies. Companies like Symantec, McAfee, Check Point Software and SonicWall fall into this category. They believe there's a long-term opportunity in the security market and are buying up technologies to create an end-to-end solution around security. They're securing networks and systems, and in some cases provide managed services around security. Their strategy consists of getting larger clients to buy into the overall data protection strategy they provide.

Corporate giants. Companies like Microsoft, Cisco and EMC believe security should be built right into their products. If they're building VoIP technology, they don't go to a third party to secure it; they use built-in security and perhaps upgrade to stronger built-in security features. This goes against the second group of manufacturers; both types of companies are buying the first group (the small technology companies).

Understanding the Vendor Security Strategy

A few years ago, Network Associates provided clients with a line of products that seemed to have no connection. Network analyzers, helpdesk software, antivirus, encryption and other offerings in a single portfolio gave buyers end-user tools, enterprise management, mid-market call centers and home user security. In 2004, the company began transforming itself, renaming products under the McAfee brand.

With management changes, the company divested of Magic, Sniffer and other products that didn't seem to fit. The new company began focusing on security, with acquisitions of Entercept intrusion prevention, Foundstone enterprise scanning and a number of other technologies, giving McAfee a full suite of security offerings from the desktop anti-x market, network access control (NAC), access control and managed services. McAfee developed offerings for the enterprise, with clients like Cisco Systems, the mid-market, SMB and even home users. Its stock went up 40 percent, and execs began to aggressively reengineer their channel.

EMC did the same thing when it added RSA and Network Intelligence to its portfolio. With the tools to store and back up data, it added security tools for monitoring and access control to drive a stronger security value proposition. EMC went from being a software company to a business continuity company and, finally, a full security company in 2006. In addition, archiving tools for email were added, building on the information life-cycle management message for data security.

BMC Software followed suit after picking up Remedy and Magic (acquired from Network Associates). With the information technology infrastructure library (ITIL) gaining importance and the announcement of ISO 20000, business services management and security merged. Identity management, change control and the role of the configuration management database (CMDB) in business continuity gave the company a security story and added to BMC's growing list of "Routes to Value" (a security value proposition).

Finally, there's Cisco. I was sitting in a meeting with thousands of partners back in the mid-'90s, as Cisco announced its three core areas of focus. At that time, the company didn't list security as a focus area, and companies like Check Point Software and ISS were really heating up.

Two years later, Cisco finally announced security as a focus area and, since that announcement, has picked up numerous security companies to create a compelling portfolio of security products.

A few years later, I found myself running a national security practice for a global integrator. As a Cisco partner, I was invited to its security VAR council. All of us were struggling to realize any recognizable profit on network security products and were waiting to hear where this company was going to take us. Cisco's strategy was clear: It was building security into the network—a strategy that would ultimately render external network security solutions like ISS obsolete.

Sure enough, by 2006, ISS was struggling to grow its business, not having licensed its software to the networking companies. IBM eventually announced its intentions to buy ISS.

The trends are evident: Security will be part of the infrastructure and part of an overall security strategy. Selling point products will result in long, unprofitable sales cycles. With this in mind, it's important for resellers to take the strategies of the companies for which they resell, justify action with the assessment tools we have discussed and create a vision in the customer's mind that leverages the entire security solution provided by a single vendor or group of partnering vendors. At some point, infrastructure companies will be incorporating baseline security tools right into their products. This is the vision that should be created.

Reseller Business Models

Resellers use many different models, some stronger than others. In general, the channel is weak in its ability to sell high-end security solutions. This is not to say that strong boutique security companies, large global integrators or companies coming from the Big Six don't exist. But the percentage is low in the general reseller population or among those who would be classified by manufacturers as partner resellers.

If you were to look at the number of North American companies that advertise security offerings on their websites and then talk to each one about its actual security project experience, you would find a lack of expertise and real-life project experience. Let's look at some of the models and who's selling security solutions. We can then consider what your firm might look like, or how you can begin building or reengineering your company to achieve greater results.

Product Versus Services

Before diving into types of resellers, it's helpful to classify your organization on a continuum—from pure product to visionary consulting. The idea is to get a sense of where your organization really sells. Is it primarily commodity (product)? In this case, you would fall in the middle or slightly left of the diagram below.

Product	Resources	Projects	Strategy	Vision

A visionary company may be like the Chasm Group, made popular in Geoffrey Moore's book *Crossing the Chasm*, which helps companies explore where they're headed, where profitability exists and how to create direction to get there. This falls to the extreme right.

Companies that fall between these two classifications include staff augmentation or resources provided to existing project teams or operations functions. Projects would include companies that focus largely on fixed-start and end initiatives, owning the overall scope, development, design, testing and turnover. Strategy may help companies develop their methodology, process and workflow. My company would most likely fall between Strategy and Vision, as I work with business owners to develop a company vision, but take them down to a tactical planning process to develop solutions strategies, offerings and sales-team enablement.

If I look primarily at the reseller population, most companies fall somewhere between resource and project. If you are like most, you are working toward more projects, but actually selling more product-install business.

Security business is best sold when your company is positioned as a strong project company. Security is then recommended and built into the projects you design and implement. Wherever there's a project initiative with a goal of providing greater functionality, operational efficiency or enhanced profitability, there is an opportunity to look at risk and remediation on the infrastructure side.

In the following subsections, I have taken the classic VAR model and created several subcategories to further define what's successful.

SMB VARs

The smaller VARs, all buying through distribution, generally treat security as a firewall sale. Clients are mostly SMB companies with less than 50 users, with limited buying power. Most of these companies have relegated themselves to break/fix work, network fileserver resales and small networking projects. The majority of revenue comes from PC hardware and repair work.

This group should not be fooled. There is a big security opportunity out there for companies of this size. Your overhead is low (at least it could be), your sales cost is low if you structure your business appropriately, and your sales cycle is short if you sell the right things. Managed services is the place to take this business, and security is the primary driver. When I refer to "security," I mean system availability, data integrity and the ability to restore quickly. The client base generally lacks IT staffing or has a low level of quality IT support.

The message is simple: Stop focusing on products, and turn everything into a managed offering. Sell the product, but trade the upfront margin for the ongoing contract. The big companies can't afford to take this business, yet it can be very profitable for the company that maintains a very small or no sales force, with low overhead.

Mid-Size VARs

The mid-size reseller has some challenges unique to this market. In general, this group has tried to move upmarket, away from the small companies, and toward companies that actually have IT people. The IT people are generally not well educated in high-tech infrastructure and information security, so there is an important role; however, IT tends to be territorial in this market.

The security opportunity still exists. Again, it is in the managed services area, but the sale is more difficult. In the SMB market, we had end users without the appropriate support. Influencers are generally willing to create introductions to the decision makers to get the support they need. In this market, you don't have that luxury. Somehow, you have to move up to the decision makers without being delegated downward. Most IT sales are going to be product resale with low margins. Your only hope is to target data owners, convincing them that security is highly specialized and not worth risking with their internal IT group. In most cases, you will be telling the truth.

The limiting factor comes in the integrator's willingness to train and invest in higher-end resources with consulting capabilities and business acumen. Remember: Policy drives architecture, so if your firm can't work in the policy area, chances are you'll be cut out of these higher-end deals.

My recommendation here is to market through executive-only,

invitation-only events. Bring in a speaker, talk about assets and risk, and get buy-in at the top before challenging existing mid-market IT thinking.

Large Integrators

They might not all be global, but I'm referring to the larger resellers that generally span multiple geographies. These resellers typically sell everything from enterprise storage to mid-range systems, larger network deployments and perhaps applications.

This group generally looks for the bigger opportunities, as overhead is high and the quota requirement demands high-involvement projects. In doing this, a couple of issues arise. First, selling product-install at this level doesn't produce enough profit to create a return on the sale (ROS), unless the accounts are very large and are buying huge quantities of products, making the cost of sale per box low. In other words, there is no net profit once the cost of selling is factored in for the first products sold. As a result, many salespeople steer away from security sales, thinking of security as a firewall with little margin.

Another issue is the larger companies' willingness to hire specialized security consultants. Great security consultants often demand higher pay than in other niche areas.

As a result, corporate managers skimp on security skills, favoring generalists in the networking group to carry out specialized assignments like security assessment work. The result should be apparent: The assessment becomes a list of network vulnerabilities routed straight to the network administrator's desk. Remediation projects never materialize, and people wonder why security is hard to sell.

The solution: Hire people with consulting skills, security experience and an interest in the bigger security picture. Focus on business continuity, security assessments and risk analysis, and move things toward a security managed services offering with reoccurring revenue potential.

Security Boutiques

I am convinced security boutiques exist because of the issues raised in the last section—primarily pay. I can think of at least five companies started by people who once worked for me, under the umbrella of a larger company. The larger company was unwilling to meet their salary requirements, so they left to form new companies focused solely on security. To my knowledge, they are all profitable and growing their bottom line. In addition, I am coaching more than one entrepreneurial team as they ramp up new security-oriented companies. I expect them to succeed.

These companies are doing well because there's a market for people who understand the value of assets, the risk associated with today's corporate computing environments and the need companies have to extend their enterprise to places they needn't go in the past. They are good at demonstrating value and showing their clients how to defend against today's cyber-criminals, and they are selling value to the data owner. In every case, this is a recipe for success.

Resellers can duplicate this within their existing business structure if they take the appropriate steps. Most of the puzzle is solved by getting the right people and empowering them.

Managed Services Companies

The last group is fairly new, as they're resellers who primarily offer managed services. They are, in fact, security companies if they sell managed-services offerings in an effective way.

Resellers have bought into the idea that managed services offer a new opportunity for margin as products commoditize; however, many of these companies are not succeeding.

Why?

There are several reasons, First, they are not selling managed services as a security sale, but as a monitoring sale. There is little value in monitoring just for the sake of monitoring. Decision makers are looking for risk reduction. Somehow, these companies must measure need and then demonstrate a reduction in risk.

Second, managed services are a hard sell to new clients. Projects are the best way to lead into new accounts, followed by managed services or some form of monthly reoccurring revenue.

The Foundation of a Winning Security Provider

Regardless of whether you're a solution provider reseller or a manufacturer, there are certain principles that make a winning approach.

Focus on Assets, Not Products. Asset-level conversations directly address the needs of the buyer. Anything else gets delegated to non-decision makers, creating an endless sales cycle.

Silo Versus Integrated. Treating security as one of your offerings makes it a product sale. An asset sale must be integrated into another solution that addresses a business need. This is where assets are created and used, and where liability and justification are found.

Request Response Versus Need Creation. Responding to RFPs means you are responding to a security sale that was actually made by someone else; it's now down to a price decision. To win, you must change the rules, expose risks, create a vision for what could be done and seize the opportunity to advise asset owners—a job worth paying for.

Buy and Sell Versus Sell and Build. Companies that buy or make products are selling the commodity. The company that creates the vision and customizes security according to the impact versus likelihood graph is worth hiring.

Engineers Versus Security Specialists. Even though a silo approach is discouraged, you still need experts to understand the risk. This is where boutique security companies have won large accounts without having the enormous sales presence of a global integrator. Specialization creates the foundation for the advisor.

Focus on the Group Without a Plan

Once you have a message that works, you must start contacting people. Who will you call?

The tendency is to take leads from the manufacturer. When you get a lead, your first reaction is to discover which products they seek. This is pure commodity business. Once a buyer knows what he needs and begins the process of procurement, price has become the differentiator. But these leads can be reengineered to develop strong security business.

Focus on the group that doesn't understand threats. Identify data owners within the accounts you call, and begin building a vision. Use your value statements to get their attention, and be prepared with a compelling value proposition. Begin the process of educating influencers and buyers on the trends of our times. Begin building a vision with people who have liability and are directly affected when compromises occur.

The diagram on page 147 may be helpful in understanding how to put together the various pieces presented in this book, starting with the APS (the advisory positioning statement); finding asset owners and presenting your value proposition; taking them through the house, cloud and coverage model to build the vision; and finally using the assessment to create justification.

In *Solution Selling,* Michael Bosworth encourages readers to focus on what he assumes to be 95 percent of the market: people who do not have a vision of what they need. He goes on to describe the other 5 percent as people who understand their organizations' needs and who are looking for products based on price. Competition already exists, and the sales cycle can be tough, especially if you're late to the party.

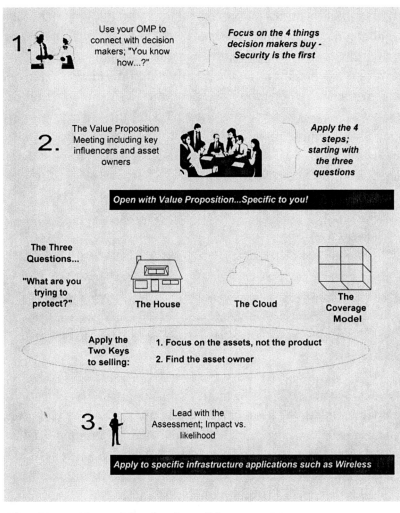

The Two-Year Marketing Plan

Do these principles guarantee a win? Nothing is a sure thing. We're dealing with people, not machines. It's impossible to predict what people will do. Many factors influence how managers and executives respond to your message. This doesn't mean you should throw everything away.

People need a vision. Start with a strong APS (Advisor Positioning Statement), and begin collecting the information you need to remain in contact with them. Use your contact database to group similar prospects or clients—those who may be interested in the same information. Then, start collecting information as you read, interact with others and learn about new industry trends.

Think of yourself as a coach, providing information that will help people make better business decisions. Rather than pestering them with weekly phone calls, asking them if they're ready to buy something, begin providing value to them. Don't overwhelm them with spam. Use a timely, methodical approach to send them targeted information. I call these efforts "idea emails." Here's an example:

> Hi, Sue:
>
> Over the last few months, I have been working with a few companies similar to yours on migrating VoIP. Given recent trends in data theft, I want to share some ideas I have with you. I would like to set up a short call—perhaps next Tuesday or Thursday, if this works for you. Please let me know if you have a few minutes, and I'll give you a call.

Next, I send hundreds of these emails, hoping only a few people will respond. With a database of about 2,500 contacts, I send notes to people who fall into all of my defined groups. It takes time to build this database, but with the APS it doesn't take too long. Every week, someone emails me in response. I have basically eliminated cold-calling through this process.

Follow these guidelines for email success:

- Short message
- No marketing language
- No sales jargon
- No acronyms or tech talk
- Not written in HTML (like a marketing letter)
- Casual and personal
- Addressed to an individual—not a group—so it appears to be the only email I've sent

- Aimed at raising curiosity about a specific topic that's relevant to my prospect
- Proposes two time slots to hundreds of people; not left open-ended
- Doesn't beg for the meeting; sounds confident
- Foreshadows that you have something to say when meeting occurs

I use my mail/merge function to create a customized email that's addressed to individuals, and I contact them nine times over the next 18 months (about every other month). My messages don't show up as spam, nor am I giving away the email addresses of others I'm contacting. The last thing you want is an email with 100 addresses. It's unprofessional.

Combine this with events using industry experts on relevant security topics, which target asset owners.

Over time, if you are providing valuable information, people will keep you in mind when issues come up. New applications, business expansion and strategy meetings will become opportunities. As people respond to my emails each week, they frequently apologize for ignoring the many messages I've sent over the months, indicating the last one hit them and they're ready to talk. If this happens weekly, your cold-calling efforts will become unnecessary.

Start today with your APS, and begin collecting as many contacts as you can in a given quarter. Track how these relationships progress. Is your question effective? Did you connect with this person? Is there an opportunity to stay in contact with relevant information?

If so, you are bound to have success in using the principles in this book to drive your security business. Remember: Security is not a product; it's a discipline. Use it to attract people who make decisions and have the liability. Upon positioning yourself as a trusted advisor, sell them the products and services your company is developing to meet the needs of today's businesses.

Summary

☑ Stop selling product. Focus on assets and sell the security vision.

☑ Understand and sell the security strategy—a long-range road-map to asset security.

☑ Build a message that fits with your business model.

☑ Target asset owners who don't understand the problem. Position yourself as the advisor, and create the vision.

☑ Use the two-year marketing plan to eliminate cold calling.

☑ Remember: Security is one of the four things. Use it to sell every technology your company offers.

About the Author

David H. Stelzl, CISSP, a preeminent expert on digital asset protection strategies, is a dynamic speaker and information security professional who inspires audiences by showing them how to use the concepts of risk and risk mitigation to develop stronger value and competitiveness in the technology sales process.

While David is a well-known expert in the field of information security, his passion is in helping organizations find lasting answers to technology sales profitability, which he shares through writing, speaking and consulting. In international workshops, he brings life to the concepts of information security, systems, networks and relevant IT/business solutions, providing simple analogies that allow technology companies to create new offerings, position commoditizing products and increase the value they bring to the end-user customer.

David is a frequent speaker at reseller marketing events, manufacturers' and distributors' channel partner events, and internal sales meetings. He has worked closely with major technology providers like Cisco Systems and Ingram Micro, and has been sponsored by companies including Hewlett Packard, IBM, RSA, Citrix and many other globally recognized technology leaders. In 2006, David's well-known workshops on selling security were required training for hundreds of technology sales representatives across America.

Prior to his consulting and speaking career, David worked and managed several technology reseller companies. Most recently, he started and ran the Security Practice for Dimension Data, North America, PLC.

Need additional copies of this book?

You may order additional copies of this book by visiting the author's website: www.stelzl.us.